THE GOURMET COOKBOOK FOR ASTROLOGY LOVERS

by

Peter Marks

with Angela Dellafiora Ford

ISBN 978-1-945907-96-8

The Gourmet Cookbook For Astrology Lovers

Author: Peter Marks

Contributing Author: Angela Dellafiora Ford

Editor: Marla McKenna

Proofreader: Philip D'Amore

Cover Design: Marla McKenna

Cover and Interior Layout: Griffin Mill

Published by
Nico 11 Publishing & Design
Mukwonago, Wisconsin
Michael Nicloy, Publisher

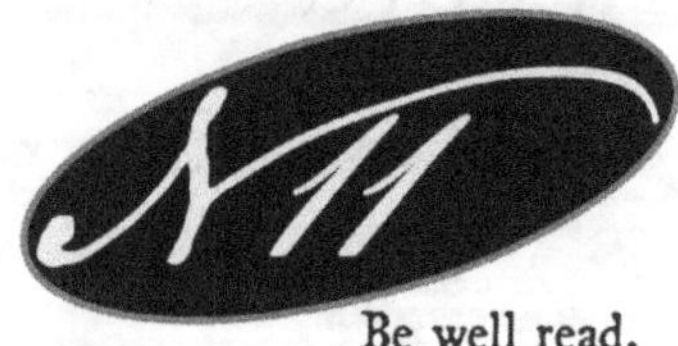

Quantity orders may be placed with the publisher via email:

mike@nico11publishing.com

Printed in the United States of America

This book is dedicated to my late mother Ruth Edith Marks, who taught me to believe in myself.

And to my Aunt Joan Hickok, who introduced me to astrology at a young age.

TABLE OF CONTENTS

INTRODUCTION

We all know there are 12 different sun signs of the zodiac. Our zodiac sign, along with hereditary and environmental factors, determines our personality, our compatibility with others, and, in general, who we are. The 12 different signs also govern the various parts of the body. For instance, Leo rules the heart, and Libra rules the kidneys. The 12 different signs make up one body. Our sun sign dictates the most vital parts of our bodies that can also be our health vulnerabilities. Why shouldn't you determine which foods are best for you when you consider this?

Before I continue, I would like to add that there are many other planetary elements that astrologers look at other than the basic sun sign that makes up our personality and influences our lives. We were all born with ascendants or rising signs and moon placements. Our ascendants can tell us much more about our personality, while moon placements explain our emotional makeup. In this book, I am only dealing with the sun sign because it is the most effective way of understanding how our life can be influenced by what we consume.

As an intuitive, psychic, and practicing astrologer for 23 years, I know the patterns between personality, body, and food. However, my association with Bob Lape, a food critic, and award-winning journalist, inspired my interest in food. I met Bob in the early 1990s when I was the producer of the TV show, *Today's Gourmet, Bob Lape*. I later worked with Bob on a travel and food show called *America Coast to Coast*. As I worked with Bob, I developed a taste for some rare and exotic dishes that you can find in this book. I am grateful to Bob because he gave me the experience of a lifetime. I learned the alchemy of cooking and food presentation from him.

This book combines two passions in my life: astrology and food. This book has 12 chapters. Each chapter discusses each sun sign's personality and how it relates to their preferred tastes regarding food. Each sun sign has its food guide and delicious recipes. You don't have to just cook the recipes according to your sign. You can try any or all the recipes if you wish. It is not a health cookbook in the traditional sense, but I have sought to keep the ingredients free from heavy cream, butter, and sugar. However, some recipes do have heavier ingredients in them. Please be your judge on how you want to cook. For example, if you need to adjust butter to margarine because you have high cholesterol, please do so.

My hope for you is that you receive some culinary insights into your life. I also hope my book presents you with a range of choices for eating natural, healthy meals according to the "stars."

– Peter Marks

INTRODUCTION

Aries (March 21 to April 20)

The planet Mars rules Aries. Mars is known as the "God of War" and also the "Red Planet."

The symbol for Aries is the ram. The ram is assertive and can rise to great heights.

The color associated with Aries is red. Red is associated with fierceness.

Aries is a cardinal fire sign. Cardinal signs are action-oriented and initiators. Fire signs are active and spontaneous. Aries people are energetic and motivated by enthusiasm.

Aries is a positive masculine sign.

Aries rules the head, face, and brain.

People born under the sign of Aries have a fiery personality and fierce determination.

They are bold, forceful, and dynamic individuals. Aries people have high energy and high stamina. They are outgoing people, and they love adventure.

Aries people are busy and active. They act quickly. They are go-getters. Movement is essential to them. Aries people have athletic bodies and excellent muscle coordination. In general, they are of average height and have good builds. Some Aries are known for their red hair and strong facial features. Aries people are rugged individuals.

Aries people are considered pioneers. The dominant keywords for Aries people are "I AM." Their dominant trait is courage. Some famous people born under the sun sign of Aries are Maya Angelou, Warren Beatty, Marlon Brando, Russell Crowe, Harry Houdini, Thomas Jefferson, Elton John, Ashley Judd, David Letterman, Steve McQueen, Eddie Murphy, Colin Powell, Gloria Steinem, Spencer Tracy, and Vincent Van Gogh.

Symbolically, Aries represents the first man, so it is quite natural that they are meat-eaters. Aries people like barbecued meat because it's red and cooked over a fire. They also like tomato-based spaghetti because it's red.

Aries people have a healthy appetite, and they need a well-balanced diet to sustain their high energy and keep their good health. A good diet for Aries consists of fish, seafood, meat, poultry, fresh salads, and natural fruit juices that keep their high metabolism under control. Aries can have a rich carbohydrate diet because it gives and sustains energy and whole-grain foods keep an Aries body full of vitality.

People born under the sign of Aries should eat foods that help keep the brain healthy. Foods that are rich in Omega-3 are known to benefit the brain. Oysters, sardines, and eggs are some foods that contain this essential fatty acid. Apples, berries, cherries, curry, cocoa, walnuts, and pumpkin seeds are good brain foods.

Proper kidney function is essential to Aries people because of the direct link to headaches and dizziness, eye strain, and earaches. Beans, brown rice, lentils, olives, lettuce, cucumbers, spinach, dried apricots, and pumpkin are beneficial to the kidneys.

Aries people are vulnerable to headaches, migraines, and sinus infections. They should eat whole-grains such as amaranth, buckwheat, and ryes to help ward off such problems. Other foods to eat that aid in preventing these types of issues are broccoli, mushrooms, potatoes, Swiss chard, almonds, sesame seeds, and yogurt.

Avocados and mangos are good fruits for Aries people to eat because they promote good eye health.

Aries people put a lot of strain on their bodies due to much physical activity. They need calcium in their bodies because it strengthens and secures their bones. They should consume dairy products and green leafy vegetables for calcium absorption. Raisins promote healthy joints and good bones. Aries people should be careful of their salt intake because it reacts negatively with their bones.

Potassium phosphate is the mineral associated with Aries. This mineral supports the liver and the brain. Aries can deplete themselves of potassium phosphate quickly because they are so active. It can cause them to be depressed. Foods rich in potassium phosphate are tomatoes, onions, cauliflower, Brussels sprouts, veal, swordfish, flounder, figs, and bananas. In addition to supporting kidney function, beans, brown rice, lentils, olives, lettuce, cucumber, spinach, dried apricots, and pumpkin are foods that also contain potassium phosphate.

Like their fiery personality, Aries people like hot spicy foods. They like different curries and chilies, and they like to put hot peppers and hot sauces on their food. Aries are adventurous when it comes to herbs and spices because they are willing to try anything for a taste of something different. Other than watching out for heartburn, Aries people tend to be very healthy, and they can eat almost anything. Cayenne, horseradish, paprika, and red pepper are some of the hot spices. Aries people like cinnamon. Basil, capers, coriander, fennel, garlic, ginger, mustard, parsley, rosemary, sage, and tarragon are just some of the many herbs and spices that please the Aries personality.

Aries people usually do not have a sweet tooth, but occasionally, they crave chocolate.

Aries people enjoy consuming all types of beverages. They are big water drinkers, and they like all different kinds of coffees and teas. They specifically like espresso and red wines.

Aries should eat their meals in a quiet, peaceful atmosphere. They should try not to be stressed out when they eat and not eat too quickly.

Aries Food Guide

Fish

Anchovy
Bass
Bluefish
Carp
Catfish
Cod
Flounder
Grouper
Haddock
Halibut
Herring
Mackerel
Mahi-mahi
Monkfish
Ocean Perch
Orange Roughy
Red Snapper
Sablefish
Salmon
Sardine
Seabass
Shark
Smelt
Snapper
Sole
Sturgeon
Swordfish
Trout
Tuna
Turbot
Whitefish
Yellowtail

Seafood

Caviar
Clams
Crab
Crayfish
Lobster
Mussels
Octopus
Oysters
Scallops
Shrimp
Squid

Meat

Bacon
Beef
Lamb
Pork
Sausage
Steak
Veal
Venison

Poultry

Capon
Chicken
Cornish Game Hen
Duck
Goose
Pheasant
Quail
Turkey

Beans (High Carbohydrates)

Black-eyed Peas
Cannellini Beans
Chickpeas
Fava Beans
Garbanzo Beans
Great Northern Beans
Green Peas
Kidney
Lentils
Lima Beans
Navy Beans
Pinto Beans
Red Beans
Split Peas
White Beans

Grains/Breads/Cereals/Pastas

Amaranth
Barley
Bran
Brown Rice
Kamut
Millet
Oats
Pumpernickel
Spelt
Wheat
Tabbouleh

Whole-Grain Foods

Buckwheat
Rye

Cheese/Dairy Products

Butter
Cheeses
Cream
Eggs
Milk
Sour Cream
Yogurt

Oils

Chile Oil
Flax Seed Oil
Fish Oil
Olive Oil
Sesame Oil
Vegetable Oil

Vegetables

Alfalfa sprouts
Artichokes
Arugula
Asparagus
Bean Sprouts
Beets
Beet Greens
Broccoli
Brussels Sprouts
Cabbage
Cauliflower
Carrots
Celery
Collard Greens
Cucumbers
Dandelion Greens
Eggplant
Endive
Green Beans
Hops
Kale
Leeks
Lettuces
Mushrooms
Mustard Greens
Okra
Onions
Parsnip
Peppers
Potatoes
Pumpkin
Radish
Rhubarb
Shallots
Spinach
Squash
Swiss Chard
Turnip
Turnip Greens
Wax Beans
Yellow Beans
Zucchini

Fruits

Apples	Cherries	Melons
Apricots	Cranberries	Olives
Avocados	Dried Apricots	Raisins
Bananas	Figs	Raspberries
Blackberries	Lemon	Strawberries
Blueberries	Lime	Tomatoes
Boysenberries	Mangos	

Herbs and Spices

Basil	Curry	Capers
Dill	Paprika	Caraway
Fennel	Parsley	Cardamom
Garlic	Red Pepper	Cayenne
Ginger	Rosemary	Chili Pepper
Horseradish	Saffron	Cilantro
Marjoram	Sage	Cinnamon
Mint	Tarragon	Clove
Mustard	Turmeric	Coriander
Nutmeg	Thyme	Cumin
Oregano		

Beverages

Coffee
Red Wine
White Wine
Espresso
Tea
Hot cocoa
Water

Other

Almonds
Walnuts

Aries Recipes

Like the Aries personality, these recipes will inspire Aries people to waste no time going to the kitchen and whip up the ingredients to make these delicious dishes. These dishes will make the Aries personalities feel like the winners they are.

Breakfast Tortilla

Serves 2

1 medium Yukon gold potato
1 Tbsp fresh chives, minced and divided
¾ tsp salt, divided
½ tsp freshly ground black pepper
4 large eggs
1 large egg white
1 Tbsp olive oil
2 cloves garlic, minced
3 Tbsp Manchego cheese, finely grated
1 tsp extra-virgin olive oil
1 cup cherry tomatoes

Preheat oven to 350 degrees Fahrenheit.

Place potato in a saucepan and cover with water. After bringing to a boil, reduce heat and simmer for 20 minutes. Potato should be tender. Drain and cool. Peel potato and thinly slice.

In a small bowl, combine 2 teaspoons chives, ¼ teaspoon salt, pepper, eggs, and egg white. Whisk the ingredients.

In an 8-inch ovenproof, nonstick skillet, heat 1 tablespoon olive oil over medium heat. Add the garlic and potato slices and cook for 30 seconds. Turn the potato gently and coat with the olive oil. Add the remaining salt.

Press the potato mixture with a spatula into a solid layer in the bottom of a tortilla pan. Pour the egg mixture over the potato mixture. Stir. Press the potato back down into bottom of pan and cook for 2 minutes. Remove from heat. Sprinkle with cheese.

Cook for 7 minutes. The center should be set. Remove from oven.

Drizzle with 1 teaspoon extra-virgin olive oil. Loosen the sides of the tortilla from pan and slide onto a serving platter. Cut into 4 wedges. Top with tomatoes and remaining 1 teaspoon chives.

Firecracker Chili

Serves 6

1 Tbsp olive oil
1 lb hamburger
3 onions, coarsely chopped
2 Tbsp chili powder
½ Tbsp ground coriander
3 14.5-oz cans diced tomatoes with green chilies
2 15.5-oz cans red kidney beans, rinsed and drained
¼ cup lightly-packed fresh cilantro leaves for garnish

Heat the olive oil in a large, nonstick skillet over medium-high heat. Stir in the hamburger and cook until browned. Transfer the hamburger to a slow cooker.

In the same skillet, add the onions and cook until soft. Remove the skillet from the heat and stir in the chili powder and coriander. Transfer the onion mixture to the slow cooker with the hamburger. Add the tomatoes and beans.

Cover and cook 4 to 6 hours on high or 8 to 10 hours on low.

Garnish with cilantro.

Pork Marrakesh

Serves 4

2 tsp olive oil
4 boneless pork chops, trimmed
¾ tsp salt
½ tsp black pepper
3 red onions, thinly sliced
12 dried apricots, sliced
1 cup unsweetened apple juice
1 ½ tsp peeled fresh ginger, minced
½ tsp dried thyme
1 cinnamon stick
½ cup fresh cilantro, chopped

Heat 1 teaspoon of the olive oil in a large nonstick skillet over medium-high heat. Sprinkle the pork chops with ¼ teaspoon of the salt and the pepper. Add the pork chops to the skillet. Cook until browned. Transfer to a plate.

Reduce the heat to medium. Add the onions, the remaining 1 teaspoon oil, and the remaining ½ teaspoon salt to the skillet. Stir and cook for 10 minutes. Onions should be golden colored.

Place half of the apricots and half of the onions in the bottom of a 5 or 6-quart slow cooker. Top the pork chops with the remaining onions and apricots. Add the apple juice, ginger, thyme, and cinnamon stick.

Cover and cook 3 to 4 hours on high or 6 to 8 hours on low. Pork should be fork-tender. When done cooking, remove the cinnamon stick.

Garnish with cilantro.

Serve with couscous.

Roasted Leg of Lamb with Mint Jelly

Serves 8

1 leg of lamb (about 3-4 lbs), trimmed
3 garlic cloves, minced
1½ Tbsp paprika
2½ tsp poultry seasoning
1 tsp salt
½ tsp pepper
4 onions, sliced
1 cup dry white wine
Mint jelly

Preheat the oven to 400 degrees Fahrenheit.

Lightly spray a roasting pan with nonstick spray.

In a small bowl, combine and stir the garlic, paprika, poultry seasoning, salt, and pepper. Add water to form a thick paste. Rub over lamb.

Place the lamb in the prepared roasting pan and top with the onions. Pour the wine into the pan. Insert an instant-read thermometer into the center of the lamb. Roast for 1 hour. Thermometer should read 145 degrees Fahrenheit.

Transfer the lamb onto a cutting board and let stand 10 minutes. Juices will set for easier slicing. Slice and serve with onions and mint jelly.

Spicy Baby Back Ribs

Serves 6 to 8

4 racks baby back ribs (about 2½ lbs each with the membrane removed from the underside of each rack)
1 cup dark brown sugar
3 Tbsp salt
1 Tbsp dry mustard
1 Tbsp ground fennel
1 Tbsp freshly ground black pepper
1 Tbsp cayenne pepper
1 Tbsp sweet smoked paprika
1 Tbsp unsalted butter
1 small onion, minced
4 cloves garlic, minced
1¼ tsp dried thyme
1¼ cups ketchup
1 cup cider vinegar
1¼ cups beef broth
¼ cup hot sauce
¼ cup Worcestershire sauce
2 Tbsp unsulfured molasses

Combine and mix the brown sugar, salt, mustard, fennel, black pepper, cayenne, and paprika into a small bowl. Sprinkle the spice mix all over the ribs, pressing and patting them. Place the ribs on 2 large rimmed baking sheets. Cover with foil and refrigerate overnight.
Preheat the oven to 250 degrees Fahrenheit.
Pour off any liquid on the baking sheets. Cover the ribs with foil and roast the meat for 3 hours. Meat should be tender. Pour off any liquid on the baking sheets.
Melt the butter in a saucepan over moderate heat. Add the onion, garlic, and thyme and cook for 5 minutes. Onion should be soft. Add the ketchup, vinegar, beef broth, hot sauce, Worcestershire sauce, and molasses and bring to a boil. Simmer over low heat for 30 minutes. Stir occasionally. Sauce should thicken.

Preheat the broiler and position a rack 10 inches from the heat.
Brush the ribs with the barbecue sauce and broil for 10 minutes. Brush and turn the ribs occasionally.

Chicken Provencal

Serves 4

1 Tbsp cooking oil

1 chicken (about 3 to 3 ½ lbs), cut into 8 pieces

1 tsp salt

½ tsp freshly ground black pepper

1 onion, chopped

3 cloves garlic, minced

¾ cup red wine

1¾ cups canned crushed tomatoes with juice

¾ tsp dried rosemary

¾ tsp dried thyme

½ cup black olives, halved and pitted

1 tsp anchovy paste

In a large deep-frying pan, heat the cooking oil over moderately high heat. Season the chicken with ¼ teaspoon salt and ¼ teaspoon pepper and put it in the pan. Cook and turn the chicken until it is browned. This should take less than 10 minutes. Remove the chicken from the pan and pour off all but 1 tablespoon of fat from the pan.

Reduce the heat to moderately low. Add the onion and garlic and cook for 3 to 4 minutes. The onion will soften a little bit. Add the wine and simmer for 2 minutes. Add the tomatoes, rosemary, thyme, olives, anchovy paste, and the remaining salt and simmer for 5 minutes.

Add the chicken thighs and drumsticks and any accumulated juices. Reduce the heat to low and cover. Simmer for 10 minutes. Add the breasts and cook the chicken for an additional 10 minutes. Add the remaining pepper.

Mango Chicken Curry Recipe

Serves 6

2 Tbsp vegetable oil
1 large onion, chopped
1 red bell pepper, chopped
2 garlic cloves, minced
2 Tbsp ginger, minced
2½ Tbsp yellow curry powder
½ tsp ground cumin
3 mangos, peeled and diced
2 Tbsp white vinegar
1 13.5-oz can coconut milk (if using low fat coconut milk, add 2 Tbsp heavy cream)
1½ lbs skinless, boneless chicken breast or thighs, cut into 1-inch pieces
½ cup raisins
Salt
Pepper
Cilantro, for garnish

Heat the oil in a large sauté pan over medium heat. Add onions and bell pepper and sauté for 4 minutes. Add the garlic and ginger and cook for an additional minute. Add the curry powder and cumin and cook for 2 more minutes.

Add the vinegar, coconut milk, and one of the three chopped mangos to the pan. Increase the heat and bring to a boil. Lower the heat and simmer for 15 minutes. Stir occasionally. Remove the pan from heat. Scoop the sauce into a blender and puree until smooth. Return the sauce to the pan.

Add the chicken pieces and raisins to the pan. Return to a low simmer. Cover the pan and cook for 10 minutes. Add the remaining chopped mangos to the pan. If using cream, stir in now. Cook uncovered at a low temperature for a minute or two. Do not let boil because the cream may curdle. Add salt and pepper to taste.

Garnish with cilantro.

Serve over rice.

Tarragon Chicken with Lemon

Serves 4

2 large lemons
4 chicken breast halves, with skin on and bone in
1½ tsp garlic, minced
1 tsp salt
4 sprigs fresh tarragon
2 Tbsp extra-virgin olive oil
¼ tsp black pepper
1 cup chicken broth
Fresh tarragon, chopped

Preheat oven to 400 degrees Fahrenheit.

Cut 1 lemon into very thin slices and juice the other. Loosen the skin of the chicken breast halves. Rub the flesh underneath the chicken with garlic and season it with half of the salt. Tuck a lemon slice and a tarragon sprig under the skin of each breast. Secure skin to breasts with toothpicks.

Place the chicken in a shallow roasting dish. Drizzle breasts with olive oil and reserved lemon juice. Scatter remaining lemon slices over chicken and season skin with the remaining salt and pepper. Pour chicken broth around chicken in the roasting dish.

Roast chicken for 40 minutes. Remove from oven. Turn broiler to high and broil chicken for 2 minutes. Chicken skin should be crispy. Remove toothpicks. Garnish with fresh tarragon.

Grilled Swordfish with Rosemary

Serves 4

½ cup white wine
4 cloves garlic, minced
2½ tsp fresh rosemary, chopped
4 swordfish steaks
¼ tsp salt
¼ tsp ground black pepper
2 Tbsp lemon juice
1 Tbsp olive oil
4 slices lemon for garnish

Preheat grill.

In an 8 x 8-inch square baking dish, stir in the wine, garlic, and 1 teaspoon of rosemary. Sprinkle the fish with salt and pepper and place in the baking dish. Coat fish on both sides. Cover. Refrigerate for at least 1 hour.

In a small bowl, combine and stir the lemon juice, olive oil, and the remaining rosemary. Set aside.

Transfer the fish to a paper towel-lined dish. Discard the marinade. Lightly oil grill grate to prevent sticking. Grill the fish 10 minutes. Turn once. Remove fish to a serving plate. Pour the lemon sauce over the fish with a spoon.

Top each fillet with a slice of lemon for garnish.

Roasted Halibut with Pepper Sauce

Serves 4

1 jar roasted red peppers, drained and chopped
18 pitted black olives, coarsely chopped
½ cup fresh basil, chopped
1 Tbsp red wine vinegar
2 Tbsp capers, drained and coarsely chopped
2 cloves garlic
2½ tsp olive oil
½ tsp salt
¼ tsp black pepper

Preheat the oven to 425 degrees Fahrenheit.

Spray a shallow roasting pan with nonstick spray.

Place the halibut in the prepared roasting pan. Brush with the olive oil. Add the salt and pepper. Roast the fish for 10 minutes. The fish should be opaque in the center.

In a serving bowl, combine and toss the roasted red pepper, olives, basil, vinegar, capers, and garlic. Pour over fish.

Mussels with Spaghetti

Serves 4

2 Tbsp extra-virgin olive oil, divided
3 large shallots, finely chopped
3 large garlic cloves, finely chopped
¼ tsp crushed red pepper
1 cup dry wine
½ cup water
2 lbs mussels, rinsed, scrubbed and debearded
12-oz package whole wheat spaghetti
1 large tomato, seeded and finely chopped
½ cup fresh parsley
½ tsp salt
Fresh ground pepper

Boil a large pot of water for cooking the pasta.

Heat 1 tablespoon of olive oil in a large pot or Dutch oven over medium heat. Add shallots. Stir and cook for 5 minutes. Add garlic and crushed red pepper. Stir and cook for 1 minute. Add wine, water, and mussels. Cover and cook for 5 minutes. When the mussels open, use tongs or a slotted spoon to transfer them to a large bowl. Discard any mussels that do not open. Reserve the mussel cooking liquid.

Meanwhile, cook the pasta in the boiling water according to package directions. Drain and return to the pot. Slowly pour the mussel cooking liquid into the pasta pot. Stir in the tomato, parsley, and the remaining tablespoon of olive oil. Season with salt and pepper.

Divide the pasta evenly among individual soup plates. Top with the reserved mussels.

Garnish with parsley.

Serve immediately.

Pesto Fettuccini

Serves 4

½ cup extra-virgin olive oil
5 garlic cloves, finely chopped
2 Tbsp dried chili flakes
1 cup bread crumbs, toasted
1 lb dried fettuccine
1½ cups grated Parmesan cheese
1 bunch fresh mint leaf

Add 6 quarts of water in a heavy pot over high heat. Boil the water and add 2 tablespoons of salt. Cook the fettuccine according to the package direction.

Heat the olive oil in a 2-quart saucepan over medium heat. Add and sauté the garlic for 8 minutes. Add the chili flakes and bread crumbs. Stir. Drain the fettuccine. Add to saucepan. Add cheese and toss. Add the mint leaves.

Serve immediately.

Curried Chicken Salad

Makes 2 to 3 Servings

4 cups nonfat plain yogurt
¼ cup olive oil or mayonnaise
1 Tbsp curry powder
2 cups cooked, cubed chicken breast
2 stalks celery, finely diced
1 cup dried cranberries
½ cup scallions, chopped
2½ Tbsp brown sugar

In a large bowl, combine yogurt, mayonnaise, brown sugar, and curry powder. Add the chicken, celery, scallions, and cranberries and toss to combine.

Grilled Chicken with Raspberry and Goat Cheese Salad

Serves 4

4 chicken cutlets
¾ tsp salt
1 bag mixed baby salad greens
2½ Tbsp raspberry vinegar
2½ tsp olive oil
½ tsp black pepper
¾ cup crumbled Goat cheese
12 oz raspberries
4 scallions, thinly sliced

Set a sprayed nonstick ridged grill pan over medium-high heat. Sprinkle the chicken with ½ teaspoon of the salt and place it on the pan. Cook the chicken for 3 minutes on each side.

In a medium bowl, combine and toss the salad greens, vinegar, oil, and the remaining salt, and pepper. Add the Goat cheese, raspberries, and scallions. Toss.

Divide the salad evenly among plates. Halve the cutlets and place 2 pieces on top of each salad.

Baked Apples with Cinnamon

Serves 4

4 medium apples
4 Tbsp brown sugar
½ tsp ground cinnamon

Preheat oven to 350 degrees Fahrenheit.

Cut out the stem and core of each apple. Leave the bottom intact. This will create a small hole in the center of each apple.

Place the apples into an 8 x 8-inch glass baking dish. Fill each apple with 1 tablespoon brown sugar and sprinkle with cinnamon. Cover with foil and bake for 1 hour. Apples should be soft.

Cool before serving.

Bananas Foster

Serves 4

1-pint vanilla or cinnamon ice cream
4 bananas, peeled, halved and sliced diagonally
1 Tbsp butter or margarine
½ cup dark brown sugar
1 cinnamon stick
¼ cup Bacardi rum
1 oz banana liqueur
Caramel sauce

Set ice cream out to soften.

Sauté the bananas in the butter or margarine in a skillet over low heat. Bananas should be brown on both sides. Add the cinnamon stick and brown sugar. Mix. Add the rum and banana liqueur. Stir for 5 minutes until bananas are smooth and bubbly. Simmer for 1 minute.

Scoop ice cream into bowls and top with bananas and caramel sauce.

Chocolate Fondue

Serves 4

1 lb bittersweet chocolate, coarsely chopped
2 Tbsp unsalted butter, cut up
1 cup water
½ cup milk
1½ Tbsp corn syrup (can substitute light corn syrup)
1 Tbsp flavored liqueur such as cherry, orange, coffee, or raspberry, (optional)
Pound cake, toasted and diced, for dipping
Assorted fruit such as whole strawberries or chunks of pineapple or pear, for dipping
½ cup almonds, toasted and finely chopped (optional)

Combine and mix chocolate and butter in a large microwavable bowl. Microwave on medium for 2 minutes. Whisk until smooth.

In a small saucepan, heat the water, milk, and corn syrup over medium-high heat. Bubbles should appear around the edge of the pan. Add this mixture into the chocolate mixture. Whisk or stir until smooth.

Arrange fruit on a large platter. Spoon fondue into a small bowl. Place almonds in another small bowl. With toothpicks, dip fruit into fondue, then into almonds.

Taurus (April 21 to May 20)

Taurus is ruled by the planet Venus. Venus is the planet of harmony, love, beauty, and music.

The symbol for Taurus is the bull. The bull is strong and stubborn. For as fierce as the bull can be, this animal can be just as gentle.

The color associated with Taurus is pink. Pink is a soft color often associated with love.

Taurus is a fixed earth sign. Fixed signs are sustaining and resistant to change. Earth signs are known to be practical and stable. Taurus people like to maintain the status quo.

Taurus is a negative feminine sign.

Taurus rules the throat, neck, and thyroid gland. It includes the vocal cords, tonsils, and palate.

People born under the sign of Taurus are earthy, solid, and grounded people. Like the bull, Taurus people are determined and have great perseverance. Being an earth sign, they are conservative, and they like tradition. Taurus people have their feet securely planted in the physical world and know what it takes to make money and live the good life. They love luxury and tend to overindulge in the pleasures of life.

Like the bull, people born under the sign of Taurus have fully developed bodies. They are robust. Taurus people can have long, expressive necks. They can also have melodious speaking voices and are good singers.

Even though Venus's influence over Taurus people gives them an exceptional creative ability, Taurus does represent material gain. The dominant keywords for Taurus people are "I HAVE." Their dominant trait is dependability. Some famous people born under the sign of Taurus are Cher, George Clooney, Perry Como, Ella Fitzgerald, Liberace, Rod McKuen, Jack Nicholson, Al Pacino, Anthony Quinn, James Stewart, Barbara Streisand, Uma Thurman, and Orson Wells.

Taurus people move slowly and steadily like the bull. They prod along. Even though Taurus people have great physical strength and good stamina, they are sluggish and dislike exercise. They tend to be sedentary. Taurus people need to be coaxed to exercise moderately.

It is easy for Taurus people to overeat and put on weight because they have a problem with moderation. They are not picky eaters because no one enjoys food more than them. They enjoy food so much because their taste buds are the most acutely sensitive out of all the zodiac signs. Taurus people are known as the gourmet eaters of the zodiac. Their diet, however, should be low in starch, fat, carbohydrates, and sugar. They should stay away from fatty and heavy foods.

Taurus people like hearty meals like beef, lamb, veal, and poultry. They do well when they eat foods high in protein which helps their sluggish metabolism. The sign of Taurus rules butter, and when used in moderation, it strengthens the bull.

Thyroid functioning is crucial to Taurus people because it can cause weight problems if it is not functioning correctly. Taurus people should eat fish and seafood because the natural iodine found in these foods will help support the thyroid. Pumpkins, cauliflower, cucumber, and peas are good foods that support the thyroid.

Taurus people are vulnerable to colds, coughs, sore throats, laryngitis, swollen glands, tonsillitis, and earaches. Foods that Taurus people should eat to ward off such vulnerabilities are apples, avocados, bananas, broccoli, carrots, garlic, grapefruit, strawberries, tomatoes, and yogurt.

Sodium sulfate is the mineral associated with Taurus. It regulates the amount of water in a person. It is found in the liver, pancreas, and the hormones of the kidney. Bloating and the feeling of being waterlogged are caused by an imbalance of this mineral inside a person's system. Asparagus, beets, celery, Swiss chard, spinach, onions, horseradish, cranberries, and raw nuts are foods that contain this mineral. In addition to supporting the thyroid, cauliflower, cucumber, and pumpkin also aid in preventing water retention. Taurus people should drink plenty of water to keep their system flushed out.

Taurus people gravitate to herbs and spices as they gravitate to food. It's like their taste buds cry out for all the different flavors and textures that the various condiments can give them. Hearty meals should be flavored with herbs such as parsley, mint, and thyme so the Bull can savor exquisite flavors. Taurus people also have a sweet tooth. Cinnamon, nutmeg, and marshmallow work well with the Taurus system. Clove, sorrel, and spearmint are other excellent choices for the Taurus palate. Some other herbs and spices that Taurus enjoy are basil, dill, caraway, chili peppers, curry, fennel, ginger, marjoram, mustard, lemon thyme, and sage.

Taurus people are born with a sweet tooth. They favor chocolate.

Due to their robust nature and vigorous constitution, Taurus people can drink almost everything. They like coffee and tea. They especially like cappuccino, and they love their wines. Taurus should drink fresh fruit juices because it can keep them cleaned out.

Taurus people like company when enjoying their large, healthy, gourmet meals.

Taurus Food Guide

Fish

Anchovy
Bass
Bluefish
Carp
Catfish
Cod
Flounder
Grouper
Haddock
Halibut
Herring
Mackerel
Mahi-mahi
Monkfish
Ocean Perch
Orange Roughy
Red Snapper
Sablefish
Salmon
Sardine
Sea Bass
Shark
Smelt
Snapper
Sole
Sturgeon
Swordfish
Trout
Tuna
Turbot
Whitefish
Yellowtail

Seafood

Caviar
Clams
Crab
Crayfish
Lobster
Mussels
Octopus
Oysters
Scallops
Shrimp
Squid

Meat

Bacon
Beef
Lamb
Liver
Pork
Sausage
Steak
Veal
Venison

Poultry

Capon
Chicken
Cornish Game Hen
Duck
Goose
Pheasant
Quail
Turkey

Beans (High Carbohydrates)

Black-eyed Peas
Cannellini Beans
Chickpeas
Great Northern Beans
Green Peas
Kidney
Navy Beans
Pinto Beans
Red Beans

Fava Beans
Garbanzo Beans
Lentils
Lima Beans
Split Peas
White Beans

Grains/Breads/Cereals/Pastas

Amaranth
Barley
Bran
Brown Rice
Kamut
Millet
Oats
Pumpernickel
Spelt
Wheat
Tabbouleh

Whole-Grain Foods

Buckwheat
Rye

Cheese/Dairy Products

Butter
Buttermilk (low fat)
Cheeses (low fat)
Cream (low fat)
Eggs
Milk (low fat)
Sour Cream (low fat)
Yogurt (low fat)

Oils

Chile Oil
Fish Oil
Flax Seed Oil
Olive Oil
Peanut Oil
Safflower Oil
Sesame Oil
Vegetable Oil

Vegetables

Alfalfa Sprouts
Artichokes
Arugula
Asparagus
Bean Sprouts
Beets
Beet greens
Broccoli
Brussels Sprouts
Cabbage
Cucumbers
Dandelion Greens
Eggplant
Endive
Green Beans
Hops
Kale
Leeks
Lettuces
Mushrooms
Peppers
Potatoes
Pumpkin
Radish
Shallots
Spinach
Squash
Swiss Chard
Turnip
Turnip Greens

Cauliflower
Carrots
Celery
Collard Greens
Mustard Greens
Okra
Onions
Parsnip
Wax Beans
Yellow Beans
Zucchini

Fruit

Apples
Apricots
Avocados
Bananas
Blackberries
Blueberries
Boysenberries
Cherries
Cranberries
Grapefruit
Lemon
Lime
Mangos
Melons
Olives
Pears
Plums
Raspberries
Strawberries
Tomatoes

Herbs and spices

Basil
Capers
Caraway
Cardamom
Cayenne
Chile Pepper
Cilantro
Cinnamon
Clove
Coriander
Cumin
Curry
Dill
Fennel
Garlic
Ginger
Horseradish
Lemon Thyme
Marjoram
Marshmallow
Mint
Mustard
Nutmeg
Oregano
Paprika
Parsley
Red Pepper
Rosemary
Sage
Sorrel
Spearmint
Tarragon
Turmeric
Thyme

Beverages

Coffee
Cappuccino
Fresh fruit juices
Red Wine
Tea
White Wine
Water

Other

Raw Nuts

Taurus Recipes

Taurus people should find much enjoyment in these recipes since they appreciate the good things in life. The many different herbs and spices found in the many different kinds of dishes will satisfy their healthy palette.

Corn and Green Chile Frittata

Serves 4

6 large eggs
1 cup frozen corn kernels, thawed
1 4.5-oz can chopped mild green chilies, drained
½ cup fat-free milk
½ tsp dried thyme
¼ tsp salt
¼ tsp pepper
2 dashes hot pepper sauce
12 cherry tomatoes, halved

In a large bowl, combine and whisk the eggs, corn, chills, milk, thyme, salt, black pepper, and pepper sauce.

Spray a medium skillet with nonstick spray and place over medium heat. Add the egg mixture and sprinkle with the tomatoes. Cover and cook for 15 minutes.

Cut the frittata in 4 wedges. Serve hot, warm, or at room temperature.

Beef Eye Round Au Jus

Serves 12

1 beef eye round roast, trimmed (about 4 ½ lbs)
1½ tsp salt
½ tsp dried thyme
¼ tsp ground black pepper
3 Tbsp olive oil
1 bag carrots, peeled and cut into 2 inches by ¼ inch matchstick strips
1 lb leeks, white and light green parts cut into 2 inches by ¼ inch matchstick strips
5 cloves, thinly sliced
1¾ cups dry red wine
¾ cup water

Preheat oven to 450 degrees Fahrenheit.

In a small bowl, combine and mix the salt, thyme, and pepper. Rub on roast.

In 10-inch skillet, heat the olive oil over medium-high heat until it is very hot.

Add the beef. Cook for 10 to 12 minutes. Beef should be brown on both sides. Transfer the beef to a medium roasting pan. Insert an instant-read thermometer into the center of the roast.

Add carrots, leeks, and cloves to the 10-inch skillet. Cook and stir for 7 or 8 minutes. Carrots should be tender. Arrange this vegetable mixture around the beef.

Roast the beef for 25 minutes. Add wine and water to the roasting pan. Turn the oven down to 325 degrees Fahrenheit. Roast the beef for an additional 45 minutes. Thermometer should read 140 degrees Fahrenheit.

Transfer roast to a large platter and let stand 15 minutes. Juices will set for easier slicing. Slice the roast into thin slices. Serve with vegetables.

Florentine Beefsteak

Serves 4

1½ inch thick T-bone steaks, (about 4 lbs)
2 Tbsp olive oil
2 tsp salt
½ tsp fresh, ground black pepper
Lemon wedges, for serving

Light the grill.

Rub the steaks with the olive oil. Sprinkle with salt and pepper.

Grill the steaks over high heat for 6 minutes. Turn occasionally. Cook the steaks longer if too rare.

Serve with lemon wedges.

Prime Rib with Garlic

Serves 10 to 12

1 prime rib roast (about 10 lbs)
10 cloves garlic, minced
2½ Tbsp olive oil
1½ tsp salt
2 tsp ground black pepper
2½ tsp dried thyme

Preheat the oven to 500 degrees Fahrenheit.

Place the roast in a roasting pan with the fatty side up. Insert an instant-read thermometer into the center of the meat.

In a small bowl, combine and mix the garlic, olive oil, salt, pepper, and thyme. Spread the mixture over the fatty layer of the roast. Sit at room temperature for no more than 1 hour.

Bake roast for 20 minutes. Reduce the temperature to 325 degrees Fahrenheit and roast for an additional hour. Thermometer should read 145 degrees Fahrenheit.

When done, let the roast sit for 10 minutes before carving. Meat will be able to retain its juices. Slice.

Chicken and Mushrooms

Serves 4

4 skinless boneless chicken breasts
½ tsp salt
¼ tsp black pepper
2 tsp olive oil
½ lb mixed mushrooms, halved
1 onion, chopped
2 carrots, chopped
1 celery stalk, chopped
3 garlic cloves, minced
1 tsp herbes de Provence
1 Tbsp all-purpose flour
1½ cups chicken broth
1 cup dry white wine
2 Tbsp fresh parsley, chopped
4 cups cooked whole wheat fettuccine

Sprinkle the chicken with the salt and pepper. Heat 1 teaspoon of the oil in a large nonstick skillet over medium-high heat. Add the chicken and cook for 8 minutes. Turn occasionally. Chicken should be brown. Transfer to a plate.

Add the remaining 1 teaspoon of oil and the mushrooms to the skillet. Cook for 5 minutes. Stir occasionally. Mushrooms should be brown. Add the onion, carrot, celery, garlic, and herbes de Provence. Cook for 3 minutes. Onion should be softened. Add the flour and stir for an additional minute. Add the broth and wine. Bring to a boil.

Return the chicken and accumulated juices to the skillet. Reduce the heat and cover. Simmer for 20 minutes. Chicken should be cooked through.

Sprinkle with the parsley and serve with the hot pasta.

Orange Roughy

Serves 4

4 orange roughy filets (6 oz each)
¼ cup bread crumbs
1½ Tbsp grated Parmesan cheese
½ tsp baking powder
½ tsp dried marjoram
½ tsp dried thyme
⅛ tsp ground red pepper
¼ tsp salt
¼ cup all-purpose flour
¼ cup low fat buttermilk
2½ tsp olive oil

Preheat the oven to 450 degrees Fahrenheit.

Coat a large baking sheet with nonstick cooking spray.

In a medium bowl, combine and mix the bread crumbs, parmesan, baking powder, marjoram, thyme, pepper, and salt.

Place the flour on a plate. Place the buttermilk in a shallow bowl. Brush both sides of the fillets with the olive oil. Dip the fish into the flour, then into the buttermilk and then into the bread crumb mixture. Place on the prepared baking sheet.

Bake for 10 to 12 minutes. The fish should be crisp, golden brown, and opaque in the center.

Salmon and Pasta Piccata

Serves 6

4 cups low fat cream or half-and-half
¾ cup butter
1 lb whole wheat fusilli pasta
1 lb salmon fillet, cooked and flaked
1 large cucumber, peeled, seeded and chopped
3 scallions, chopped
¾ cup fresh parsley, chopped
½ cup fresh dill, chopped
2 Tbsp Dijon mustard
2 Tbsp capers
1 Tbsp grated lemon rind

Heat the cream and butter over very low heat for 30 minutes. Cream mixture should be reduced by half.

Prepare pasta according to directions. Drain.

Add the remaining ingredients except the pasta to the cream mixture. Heat for 5 minutes over low heat. Stir occasionally. Add pasta.

Pour salmon sauce over pasta and serve.

Stuffed Avocado with Seafood

Serves 2

½ cup cooked crabmeat, flaked
½ cup cooked small shrimp
2½ Tbsp peeled and diced cucumber
1 Tbsp mayonnaise
1 tsp fresh parsley, chopped
1 pinch salt
1 pinch ground black pepper
1 pinch paprika
1 medium avocado

In a bowl, combine and mix the crab, shrimp, cucumber, mayonnaise, and parsley. Season with salt and pepper. Cover. Chill in the refrigerator.
Slice the avocado lengthwise, and remove the pit. Scoop out the flesh of the avocado. Leave about ½ inch on the peel. Spoon the seafood mixture into the hollowed centers of the avocado halves.

Sprinkle the tops with paprika.

Baked Ditalini with Three Cheeses

Serves 6

1 lb Ditalini or other medium or small shaped pasta
1 cup skim milk
¾ cup Ricotta cheese, part skim
½ cup low fat Sharp Cheddar cheese, grated
½ cup Parmesan cheese
2 Tbsp Parmesan cheese
½ cup fresh parsley, chopped
¼ tsp salt
¼ tsp black pepper, freshly ground
½ cup fine bread crumbs, dry
2 Tbsp melted butter
Preheat the oven to 375 degrees Fahrenheit.

Prepare the pasta according to package directions. Reduce the cooking time by one-third. Drain.

While pasta is cooking, combine the milk and Ricotta cheese in a blender. Blend until smooth. Transfer to a medium mixing bowl and stir in the Sharp Cheddar cheese, ½ cup of the Parmesan cheese, the parsley, salt, and pepper. Mix well.

Stir the pasta into the cheese mixture. Blend well. Transfer to a 10-inch round casserole dish.

Combine and mix the bread crumbs, butter, and 2 tablespoons of Parmesan cheese in a small bowl. Sprinkle mixture evenly over casserole.

Bake 35 minutes. Should be heated through, bubbling around the edges and the bread crumbs are golden brown.

Serve immediately.

Gnocchi with Braised Mushrooms and Peas

Serves 6

1½ lbs gnocchi
3 Tbsp extra-virgin olive oil
6 oz cremini or Portobello mushrooms, sliced
1½ cups beef broth
10 sprigs thyme
1 cup frozen peas, thawed
1½ Tbsp butter
3½ cups radicchio, coarsely chopped
Salt
Pepper

In a large pot of boiling, salted water, cook the gnocchi according to package directions. Drain. Transfer to a baking pan lined with a paper towel.

In a large nonstick skillet, heat 1 tablespoon olive oil over medium-high heat. Add the mushrooms and cook for 5 minutes. Mushrooms should be browned. Add the beef broth and 4 sprigs of thyme. Bring to a boil. Cook for 6 minutes. Broth should be reduced to about ¼ cup. Transfer to a medium bowl. Discard the thyme. Add the peas. Stir. Season with salt and pepper. Wipe out the skillet.

Add the remaining 2 tablespoons olive oil and butter in the skillet. Heat over medium-high heat. Add the gnocchi. Cook until golden in color. Toss occasionally. Add the radicchio and sauté for 2 minutes. Radicchio should be wilted. Season with salt and pepper.

Divide the gnocchi mixture among shallow pasta bowls. Top with the mushroom mixture and the remaining sprigs of thyme.

Acorn Squash

Serves 4

2 acorn squash
2½ Tbsp butter
¼ tsp nutmeg
½ tsp Salt
¼ tsp Pepper

Preheat oven to 450 degrees Fahrenheit.

Spray a 15½ x 10½ inch jelly-roll pan with nonstick cooking spray.

Cut each squash lengthwise in half. Scoop out the seeds and discard. Cut to make 8 wedges. Place squash in pan.

In a cup, combine and stir the margarine, nutmeg, salt, and pepper. Brush the sides of the squash with the margarine mixture.

Bake squash for 30 minutes. Squash should be lightly browned and fork-tender.

Grilled Asparagus with Thyme

Serves 4

2 lbs asparagus, trimmed
4 Tbsp olive oil
Fresh thyme (sprigs removed)
Salt and pepper

Add the olive oil to a bowl. Add the thyme, salt, and pepper to the bowl. Toss with the olive oil. Add the asparagus.
Grill the asparagus for 4 minutes. Turn frequently. Asparagus should be tender and brown.

Mixed Greens and Fruit Salad

Serves 6 to 8

½ cup olive
⅓ cup seasoned rice vinegar
1 Tbsp fresh lime juice
1 Tbsp minced fresh cilantro
½ tsp garlic powder
Pinch of cayenne pepper
3 cups mixed salad greens
1 Anjou pear peeled and cubed
1 avocado, pitted, peeled cubed
1 small red onion, thinly sliced
½ cup celery leaves
¾ cup crumbled Gorgonzola cheese
Salt and Pepper

In a medium bowl, combine and whisk the first six ingredients. Season with salt and pepper. Cover and refrigerate. Can be prepared 24 hours in advance.

Bring to room temperature before using. In a large bowl, combine and mix the salad greens, pear, avocado, celery leaves, and onion. Toss with dressing to coat. Sprinkle with Gorgonzola cheese.

Serve. Pass any remaining dressing separately.

Poached Pears with Wine

Serves 8

4 cups water
1½ cups dry white or red wine
1 cup sugar
Zest of lemon, removed in strips with a vegetable peeler
1 Tbsp lemon juice
4 large firm, ripe Bartlett or Bosc pears, peeled, halved, and cored

In a large sauce, add all the ingredients except the pears. Boil over high heat for 10 minutes.

Add the pears to the saucepan. Reduce the heat. Cover and simmer for 15 minutes. Pears should be tender. Transfer the pears to a large shallow bowl with a slotted spoon.

Boil the poaching liquid over high heat for 15 minutes. Should be reduced to about 2 cups. Pour the poaching liquid over the pears. Refrigerate.

Pears should be cool before serving.

S'more Cookies

Makes about 3 dozen cookies

1 cup graham cracker crumbs
1½ cups all-purpose flour
½ tsp baking soda
½ tsp salt
6 oz unsalted butter, at room temperature
½ cup granulated sugar
½ cup packed light brown sugar
1 large egg, at room temperature
½ tsp vanilla extract
1 cup semi-sweet chocolate chips
Approximately 1½ cups mini marshmallows
2 chocolate bars, coarsely chopped

Preheat oven to 350 degrees Fahrenheit.

Line two baking sheets with parchment paper.
In a medium bowl, combine and whisk the graham cracker crumbs, flour, baking soda, and salt.

With an electric mixer, cream the butter and both sugars on medium speed for 2 minutes. Add the egg and vanilla. Beat. Change the electric mixer setting to low. Add the flour mixture and beat until all ingredients are well combined. Stir in the chocolate chips.
Drop heaping tablespoons of the dough onto the prepared baking sheets. Space the balls about 2 inches apart.

Bake for 9 minutes.

Remove from oven. Gently push a few marshmallows and a couple of pieces of chocolate into the top of each cookie. Return the cookies to the oven and bake for an additional 2 to 3 minutes. Edges should be set.

Cool the cookies on the baking sheets for 5 minutes. Transfer the cookies to a wire rack to cool completely.

Strawberries and Whipped Cream

Serves 8 to 10

Approximately 35 fresh large strawberries

2 Tbsp Port sherry

1 cup confectioner's sugar

1½ cups low-fat cream

Wash strawberries in cold water. Drain. Remove the tops. Slice into quarters. Refrigerate.

Whip the heavy cream in an electric mixer at medium speed. Fold in cup of the confectioner's sugar. Add sherry. Mix well.

Serve at once or refrigerate until ready to serve.

If refrigerating, whipped cream may need to be re-whipped to stiffen.

Gemini (May 21 to June 20)

Gemini is ruled by the planet Mercury. Mercury is known as the planet of communication. In Greek mythology, Mercury is known as the messenger of the gods.

The symbol for Gemini is the twins. The twins represent duality and versatility.

The colors associated with Gemini are yellow and green.

Gemini is a mutable air sign. Mutable signs are flexible and can adjust to change. Air signs are mentally strong and intellectually oriented. The Gemini personality can adapt quickly easily to new environments and circumstances.

Gemini is a positive masculine sign.

Gemini rules the arms, hand, shoulders, and lungs, and it also governs the nervous system.

People born under the sign of Gemini have two personalities. They can do two things at one time quickly and efficiently. Geminis are both mentally and physically active people.

Mentally, Geminis are sharp-witted, intelligent, curious, clever, and quick to learn. They have a nervous temperament. Geminis have an easy time dealing with ideas and abstractions. They can gather, analyze, and disseminate information rather quickly. Geminis are usually extroverts. It is easy for them to express themselves. Geminis enjoy good conversation, and they are often chatterboxes. Geminis are entertaining.

Physically, Geminis are born with an abundance of energy. They tend to be tall and slender with long limbs. Geminis are lively and energetic, which causes them to move quickly. They like to exercise and enjoy fast-motion exercises like aerobics, jogging, or bike riding. They like to feel the air on their face. They also like to swim. Geminis are good dancers because they are light on their feet.

Gemini represents thought and communication. The dominant keywords for Gemini are "I THINK." Their dominant trait is responsiveness. Some famous people born under the sign of Gemini are F. Lee Bailey, Clint Eastwood, Ian Fleming, John F. Kennedy, Paul McCartney, Barry Manilow, Dean Martin, Bill Moyers, Prince, Walt Whitman, Venus Williams, and Frank Lloyd Wright.

Geminis have a high metabolism, and they can lose weight quickly because they are an air sign. It is difficult for Geminis to sit down and eat because they are in perpetual motion. They eat many small meals throughout the day. They like snacks and appetizers. Geminis can become junk-food addicts because they are inclined to eat on the run. They must have a proper diet to keep up their energy and maintain a positive spirit. Because Geminis are mentally stimulated, they crave various foods, and they like meals with different flavors and textures—Geminis like exotic foods.

Geminis are attracted to light foods. Their bodies have trouble digesting heavy foods. They can eat all kinds of birds. Broiled fish, seafood, lean meats, and eggs are good foods for Geminis to eat.

Geminis should eat foods that keep their lungs healthy since they are prone to upper respiratory infections, bronchitis, and asthma. Fruit such as apricots, grapefruit, oranges, and peaches help keep their lungs clean and prevent mucus, while cauliflower and lettuce help fight against bronchitis.

Because of Mercury, the ruling planet of Gemini, controlling the link between the mind and the body's functions, the Gemini brain and nervous system work continuously and tend to become overstimulated. Many types of fish such as anchovy, sardines, salmon, and scallops are good "brain foods" because they have a high concentration of Omega-3. Avocados and walnuts also contain Omega-3. Apples, bananas, carrots, celery, coconut, dried apricots, green beans, plums, prunes, spinach, tomatoes, and wheat germ have beneficial influences on the nervous system.

Like the Aries personality, Geminis are physically active. They put a lot of strain on their body. They need calcium to strengthen their bones. Dairy products such as milk, buttermilk, cheese, and green leafy vegetables are good calcium choices. Raisins help promote healthy joints.

Potassium chloride is the mineral that rules Gemini. It builds the protein fibrin in the body that aids in blood coagulation and blood circulation. Asparagus and wild rice are two foods containing high potassium chloride levels. In addition to supporting the nervous system, carrots, celery, green beans, plums, tomatoes, and spinach also contain this potassium chloride. It keeps the lungs, and bronchial tubes unclogged. Apricots, peaches, and plums, foods mentioned earlier, have potassium chloride that benefits the lungs.

Variety is the spice of life for Geminis. They like to cook with many different herbs and spices because it puts variety in their food. Anise, caraway, cardamom, clove, dill, ginger, licorice, mint, nutmeg, sesame, sage, and vanilla are some of the herbs and spices that go well in a Gemini's kitchen.

Geminis should be careful with sugar and caffeine beverages such as coffee and tea. They are naturally high-strung because they run on nerves. Stimulants can make them worse. They should drink decaffeinated herbal teas like chamomile, kava, and peppermint because of their calming effect. They should also use honey as a sweetener because it will not make them hyper. Honey also has more nutritional value than refined sugar. Geminis should drink plenty of water so that mucus will not build up in their system.

Geminis usually are not interested in alcohol with meals. They would rather amuse people with good conversation.

Gemini Food Guide

Fish

Anchovy	Mackerel	Smelt
Bass	Mahi-mahi	Snapper
Bluefish	Monkfish	Sole
Carp	Ocean Perch	Sturgeon
Catfish	Orange Roughy	Swordfish
Cod	Red Snapper	Trout
Flounder	Sablefish	Tuna
Grouper	Salmon	Turbot
Haddock	Sardine	Whitefish
Halibut	Sea Bass	Yellowtail
Herring	Shark	

Seafood

Caviar	Lobster	Scallops
Clams	Mussels	Shrimp
Crab	Octopus	Squid
Crayfish	Oysters	

Meat

Lean Red Meats	Veal	Venison

Poultry

Capon	Duck	Quail
Chicken	Goose	Turkey
Cornish Game Hen	Pheasant	

Beans (High Carbohydrates)

Black-eyed Peas	Great Northern Beans	Navy Beans
Cannellini Beans	Green Peas	Pinto Beans
Chickpeas	Kidney	Red Beans
Fava Beans	Lentils	Split Peas
Garbanzo Beans	Lima Beans	White Beans

Grains/Breads/Cereals/Pastas

Amaranth
Barley
Bran
Brown Rice
Kamut
Millet
Oats
Pumpernickel
Spelt
Tabbouleh
Wheat

Whole-Grain Foods

Buckwheat
Rye
Wild Rice

Cheese/Dairy Products

Butter
Buttermilk
Eggs
Cheeses
Cream
Milk
Sour Cream
Yogurt

Oils

Coconut Oil
Fish Oil
Flax Seed Oil
Olive Oil
Peanut Oil
Safflower Oil
Sesame Oil
Vegetable Oil

Vegetables

Alfalfa Sprouts
Artichokes
Arugula
Asparagus
Bean Sprouts
Beets
Beet Greens
Broccoli
Brussels Sprouts
Cabbage
Cauliflower
Carrots
Celery
Peppers
Cucumbers
Dandelion Greens
Eggplant
Endive
Green Beans
Hops
Kale
Leeks
Lettuces
Mushrooms
Mustard Greens
Okra
Onions
Potatoes
Pumpkin
Radish
Shallots
Spinach
Squash
Swiss chard
Turnip
Turnip Greens
Wax Beans
Yellow Beans
Zucchini
Collard Greens

Fruit

Apples
Apricots
Avocados
Bananas
Blackberries
Blueberries
Boysenberries
Coconut
Cranberries
Dried Apricots
Grapefruit
Lemon
Lime
Mangos
Melons
Nectarines
Olives
Oranges
Peaches
Pears
Plums
Pomegranate
Prunes
Raisins
Raspberries
Strawberries
Tangerines
Tomatoes

Herbs and Spices

Anise
Basil
Caraway
Cardamom
Cayenne
Cilantro
Cinnamon
Clove
Coriander
Cumin
Dill
Fennel
Garlic
Ginger
Lemon Balm
Licorice
Marjoram
Mint
Nutmeg
Sage
Sesame
Sorrel
Spearmint
Thyme
Turmeric
Vanilla

Beverages

Decaffeinated Herbal Teas
Fruit Juices
Water

Other

All Types of Nuts
Honey

Gemini Food Recipes

The versatility in these recipes should fill the versatile Gemini with total joy. The ingredients in the recipes give high energy and a healthy immune system which a Gemini needs.

Multigrain Pancakes

Serves 4 to 6

4 cups whole wheat flour

½ cup all-purpose flour

¾ cup quick-cooking oats

2 Tbsp cornmeal

2 Tbsp packed dark brown sugar

1 tsp baking powder

¼ tsp baking soda

½ tsp salt

1 cup whole milk

¼ cup plain yogurt

1 Tbsp unsalted butter, melted and cooled

1 large egg, lightly beaten

½ tsp vanilla extract

Preheat oven to 200 degrees Fahrenheit.

In a bowl, combine and whisk both flours, oats, cornmeal, brown sugar, baking powder, baking soda, and salt.

In a small bowl, whisk milk, yogurt, butter, egg, and vanilla. Stir into flour mixture.

Preheat a large skillet or griddle. Mist with cooking spray. Pour ¼ cup of batter onto the skillet or griddle. Cook for 2 minutes. Bubbles should be formed on the tops of the pancakes. The bottoms of the pancakes should be golden. Flip pancakes and continue cooking for an additional minute. Pancakes should be cooked through and golden in color.

Place the cooked pancakes on a plate, and place them in an oven on low heat. They will remain warm while cooking the remaining pancakes.

Indian Chicken with Cucumber Raita

Serves 4

1½ lbs skinless, boneless chicken breasts

1 cup low fat plain yogurt

Juice of ½ lemon

3 cloves garlic, peeled

1-piece fresh ginger, peeled and thinly sliced

½ tsp salt

½ tsp garam masala

½ tsp ground coriander

½ tsp turmeric

½ tsp sugar

Pinch cayenne

1 medium cucumber, finely diced

¼ cup fresh mint, chopped

Flatbread, toasted (optional)

In a food processor, add ½ cup of the yogurt, the lemon juice, garlic, and ginger, ½ teaspoon of the salt, the garam masala, coriander, turmeric, sugar, and cayenne. Puree. Transfer the mixture to a large zip lock bag. Add the chicken and coat. Squeeze out the air and seal the bag.

Refrigerate for at least 30 minutes or up to 24 hours. Turn the bag occasionally.

Remove the chicken from the marinade. Discard the marinade.

Preheat the broiler.

Line a baking sheet with aluminum foil. Spray with nonstick spray.

Thread the chicken on 8 12-inch skewers. Place the skewers on the prepared baking sheet. Broil 5 inches from the heat for 4 minutes on each side. Chicken should be browned and cooked through.

To make the raita, combine and stir the remaining ⅔ cup yogurt, the cucumber, mint, and the remaining ¼ teaspoon salt in a serving bowl.

Serve the raita with the chicken and flatbread.

Roasted Chicken

Serves 4 to 6

1 roasting chicken (about 7 lbs)
1½ tsp lemon balm, minced
1½ tsp marjoram, minced
2 Tbsp fresh thyme, minced
2 Tbsp extra-virgin olive oil
4 cloves garlic, chopped
4 sprigs lemon balm, for garnish
4 sprigs marjoram, for garnish
2 tsp all-purpose flour
1 lemon, quartered
½ cup dry white wine
1 cup canned low salt chicken broth
Salt
Pepper

Preheat oven to 450 degrees Fahrenheit.

Rinse chicken and pat dry. Place in a roasting pan.

In a bowl, combine and mix the lemon balm, marjoram, thyme, olive oil, and garlic. Rub 1 tablespoon of garlic-herb oil over the chicken. Add salt and pepper to the chicken.

Place the lemon, 2 sprigs of lemon balm, and 2 sprigs of marjoram in the cavity of the chicken. Tie legs with string.

Roast the chicken for 20 minutes.

Reduce oven temperature to 375 degrees Fahrenheit.

Insert an instant-read thermometer into the thickest part of the inner thigh of the chicken. Roast chicken for 1 hour and 15 minutes. Thermometer should read 180 degrees Fahrenheit. Lift and slightly tilt the chicken. Empty the juices from the chicken cavity into a pan. Transfer the chicken to a serving platter. Place aluminum foil over the chicken to keep warm.

Pour the pan juices into a large glass measuring cup. Spoon the fat off the top. Add the wine to pan and heat over high heat. Boil. Scrape up any browned bits. Pour the wine mixture into the measuring cup with the pan juices. Do not clean roasting pan. Add enough chicken broth to the cup to measure 1½ cups. Return broth mixture to same roasting pan. Mix flour into reserved 1 tablespoon garlic-herb oil. Whisk into broth mixture. Over 2 burners, boil the broth mixture in the roasting pan for 2 minutes. Mixture should thicken. Season the pan juice mixture to taste with salt and pepper. Pour into sauceboat.

Serve chicken. Pass the pan-juice mixture separately.

Linguini with Duck Legs

Serves 4

1 lb linguini

1 or 2 slow-roasted duck legs

5 cloves garlic, finely chopped

1 Tbsp butter

2 Tbsp duck fat

Salt

Freshly ground black pepper

Lemon zest

3 Tbsp lemon juice

Preheat oven to 300 degrees Fahrenheit.

Pat dry the duck legs. Prick the duck's skin with a needle. Salt all over. Place in a casserole dish. Cook for 90 minutes. Skin should pull away from the bones and be somewhat crispy.

Turn the heat up to 375 degrees Fahrenheit. Cook duck legs for 15 minutes. Duck should start to get light golden brown. Remove duck legs from oven. Cool for 15 minutes.

Pick the meat off the duck legs. Reserve the skin. Cut or tear up the meat and skin into small pieces. Melt the butter in a large sauté pan over medium-high heat. Add the duck fat, duck meat, and skin. Cook for 2 minutes. Turn the heat down to medium. Add the garlic. Turn off the heat when the garlic begins to brown.

Prepare the pasta according to package directions. Drain the pasta when it is al dente.

Turn the heat back on to medium. Toss the pasta in the sauté pan. Coat well. Add more duck fat if needed. Add the black pepper and 1 tablespoon of lemon juice. Toss. Taste. Add the second tablespoon of lemon juice if needed.

Serve immediately with the lemon zest sprinkled on top.

Fish Tacos

Serves 4

2 skinless mahi-mahi fillets (about 6 oz)

½ tsp salt

½ tsp cumin

8 small taco shells

1 avocado, halved, pitted, peeled and diced

1 cup romaine lettuce, thinly sliced

½ cup cilantro

1 lime, cut into 8 wedges

¾ cup salsa

Spray the broiler rack with a nonstick cooking spray.

Preheat the broiler.

Sprinkle the mahi-mahi fillets with the salt and cumin.

Place the fillets on the broiler rack. Broil 5 inches from the heat for 3 minutes on each side. The fish should be opaque and flaky.

Transfer the fish to a plate.

Divide the fish evenly among the taco shells. Add lettuce, avocado, and cilantro.

Serve the tacos with the lime wedges and the salsa.

Jamaican Grilled Fish

Serves 4

4 catfish fillets

3 green onions, finely chopped

1 jalapeno pepper, seeded and chopped

2 Tbsp brown sugar

2 Tbsp Worcestershire sauce

2 Tbsp white wine vinegar

1 Tbsp fresh ginger, minced

3 cloves garlic, minced

1 tsp allspice

¼ tsp dried thyme

½ tsp salt

¼ tsp black pepper

Preheat the grill at medium heat. Lightly oil the grill.

In a large bowl, combine and mix all the ingredients except the catfish. Add the fish. Coat well. Cover and let stand at room temperature for 5 to 10 minutes

Remove fillets from the bowl. Reserve the marinade.

Place the fish on the prepared grill. Brush with half the marinade. Cook for 5 minutes. Turn the fish. Brush with the remaining marinade. Cook for an additional 8 minutes. Remove from heat and serve.

Zesty Halibut

Serves 4

2 lbs halibut fillet rinsed and patted dry

1 green bell pepper, seeded and cut lengthwise into long, thin strips

1 red bell pepper, seeded and cut lengthwise into long, thin strips

1 yellow bell pepper, seeded and cut lengthwise into long, thin strips

2 small onions, thinly sliced

1 Tbsp fresh ginger, grated

2½ tsp soy sauce

½ cup freshly squeezed orange juice

½ Tbsp finely grated orange zest

2 scallions (dark green part only), chopped, for garnish

Preheat the oven to 425 degrees Fahrenheit.

Place the fish in a baking dish. Top with the bell peppers, onion, ginger, and soy sauce. Pour the orange juice over the fish. Sprinkle the zest over the fish. Cover the dish tightly with parchment paper. Bake for 15 minutes. Fish should be cooked through.

Transfer the fish to a serving platter with two large spatulas or spoons. Pour the juices from the baking dish over the fish.

Garnish with scallions and serve.

Turkey and Spinach Lasagna

Serves 9

1 Tbsp olive oil

1 medium yellow onion, chopped

4 cloves garlic

¾ lb ground turkey breast

3 cups tomato sauce (bought or homemade)

1½ cups Ricotta cheese, part skim

1 package frozen spinach (10 oz), completely defrosted and squeezed of all excess liquid

1 cup parsley, chopped

2 egg whites

¼ tsp salt

¼ tsp pepper

12 lasagna noodles

½ cup Mozzarella cheese, part skin

½ cup Parmesan cheese

Cook lasagna noodles according to package directions.

Preheat oven to 375 degrees Fahrenheit.

Heat the olive oil in a large skillet. Add the onion and stir occasionally. Cook for 7 minutes. Onion should be softened. Add the garlic. Cook 1 minute.
Add the turkey. Cook, while breaking up the turkey with a spoon, for 5 minutes. Turkey should be cooked through and no longer pink. Add tomato sauce. Bring to a boil. Reduce heat. Simmer for 3 minutes. Remove skillet from heat and cool slightly.
In a large bowl, combine and mix the ricotta cheese, spinach, parsley, egg whites, salt, and pepper.

Coat the bottom of a 14 x 11-inch lasagna pan with ½ cup of the sauce. Arrange three lasagna noodles on the bottom of the pan. Spread ¾ cup sauce evenly over noodles. Spoon ¾ cup of the ricotta-spinach mixture evenly on top of sauce. Repeat layers two more times.
Cover top with three noodles and remaining ¾ cup sauce. Sprinkle with Mozzarella and Parmesan cheeses. Cover loosely with foil and bake for 45 minutes. Remove foil and bake 10 to 15 minutes. Cheese should be bubbly.

Cut into 9 squares and serve.

Asian Shrimp Salad

Serves 4

2 lbs medium shrimp, peeled and deveined

Grated zest of 1 lime

2½ Tbsp lime juice

2 Tbsp reduced-sodium teriyaki sauce

1 jalapeno pepper, seeded and minced

3 cucumbers, sliced

1 bell pepper, thinly sliced

3 carrots, shredded

¾ cup fresh cilantro, chopped

½ cup fresh mint, thinly sliced

1 shallot, thinly sliced

½ honeydew melon, seeded and cut into wedges

Boil water in a large saucepan. Add the shrimp. Cook for 2 minutes. Shrimp should be opaque in the center. Drain the shrimp. Rinse under cold water. Drain again.

In a large bowl, combine and whisk the lime zest and juice, teriyaki sauce, and jalapeno pepper. Add the shrimp, cucumbers, bell pepper, carrots, cilantro, mint, and shallot. Toss to coat.

Serve with the melon.

Chicken Pasta Salad with Apples

Serves 4

½ cup orange juice

3 Tbsp balsamic vinegar

1 Tbsp Dijon mustard

1 Tbsp maple syrup

3½ cups whole wheat penne, cooked

1½ cups cooked chicken breast, diced

½ cup pecans, coarsely chopped

1 Granny Smith apple, cored and chopped

1 shallot, finely chopped

1 bag baby arugula (5 oz)

Prepare the pasta according to directions.

To make the dressing, combine and whisk the orange juice, vinegar, mustard, and maple syrup in a large bowl.

Add the pasta, chicken, pecans, apple, and shallot to the dressing. Toss and coat.

Divide the arugula evenly among 4 plates. Spoon the pasta salad evenly on top.

Quinoa with Toasted Pistachios

Serves 4

½ cup quinoa

¾ cup peanut oil

½ cup shelled unsalted pistachios

1 bunch scallions, chopped

½ cup dried apricots, chopped

2 tsp fresh ginger, minced

1 clove garlic, minced

1 cup chicken broth

¼ hot pepper sauce

2 Tbsp fresh cilantro, chopped

Apricots, sliced, for garnish

Place the quinoa in a fine-mesh strainer. Rinse under cold water until the water clears. Set aside.

Heat the peanut oil over medium heat in a medium saucepan. Add the pistachios. Cook and stir frequently for 3 minutes. Nuts should be golden colored. Remove the nuts to a smaller bowl with a slotted spoon.

Add the scallions, chopped apricots, ginger, and garlic to the saucepan. Cook and stir, for 2 minutes. Add the chicken broth and the hot pepper sauce. Bring to a boil. Add the quinoa and cilantro. Stir. Reduce the heat to low. Cover and simmer for 25 minutes. Liquid should be absorbed.

Remove from heat and let stand for 5 minutes. Fluff with a fork and stir in the pistachios.

Garnish with apricot slice before serving.

Tuna and White Bean Salad

Serves 4

¾ cup chicken broth

2½ tsp olive oil

Grated zest and juice of 1 lemon

½ tsp salt

¼ tsp pepper

6 cups lettuce, torn

2 different color bell peppers, chopped

1 large tomato, chopped

3 scallions, thinly sliced

2 6-oz cans water-packed solid white tuna, drained and flaked

1 15.5-oz can cannellini beans, rinsed and drained

To make the dressing, combine and whisk the broth, olive oil, lemon zest, lemon juice, salt, and black pepper in a large serving bowl.

Add the remaining ingredients to the dressing. Toss to coat. Chill before serving.

Squash Soup

Serves 4

3 lbs butternut squash, peeled, seeded and cut into ½ inch pieces

1 onion, chopped

½ tsp anise seeds

2 Tbsp butter

2 cups chicken or vegetable stock

3 cups water

Salt

Pepper

Sour cream, for garnish

Melt the butter in an 8-quart pot over medium heat. Add the squash, onion, and anise seeds. Cover and cook for 15 minutes. Stir occasionally. Add the chicken or vegetable stock, water, salt, and pepper. Cover and simmer for 30 minutes. Squash should be tender. Cool.

Add the soup in batches to a blender. Puree. Season with salt and pepper.

Garnish with a dollop of sour cream before serving.

Wild Mushroom Soup

Serves 6

2 Tbsp unsalted butter

2 Tbsp olive oil

1 medium onion, cut into medium dice

3 cloves garlic, minced

1 lb fresh wild mushrooms, wiped clean, trimmed and thinly sliced (If using shitake mushroom, remove stems)

2 Tbsp fresh thyme

1 tsp fresh thyme

½ tsp salt

½ tsp black pepper, freshly ground

4 cups chicken broth

½ cup plain Greek yogurt

4 Tbsp dry sherry (optional)

2 Tbsp soy sauce

Melt the butter and olive oil in a 5-quart pot over medium-high heat. Add the onion and cook for 4 minutes. Onion should be very lightly brown. Add the garlic. Cook for 1 minute. Add the mushrooms, 2 tablespoons of the thyme, salt, and pepper. Cook for 4 minutes. The mushrooms should be limp.

Add the chicken broth. Scrape up any browned bits in the pot with a wooden spoon. Bring to a boil over high heat. Reduce the heat. Simmer for 10 minutes. Mushrooms should be tender. Remove from heat. Slightly cool.

Add about half of the soup to a blender. Puree. Return the soup to the pot. Add the yogurt, soy sauce, and sherry, if using. Season with salt and pepper. Reheat.

Garnish each bowl with a small pinch of the remaining 1 teaspoon thyme before serving.

Carrot Bran Snack Bars

Makes 16 bars

2 cups bran cereal
1¾ cups shredded carrot
1 cup milk
½ cup drained canned crushed pineapple
½ cup Greek plain yogurt
1¾ cups whole-wheat flour
1½ tsp baking powder
¾ tsp ground cinnamon
½ tsp baking soda
½ tsp salt
1 egg
½ cup liquid honey

Preheat oven to 375 degrees Fahrenheit.

Line a 13 x 9-inch metal baking pan with aluminum foil. Leave a 2-inch overhang of the aluminum at each end of the pan. Lightly butter the foil.

In a large bowl, combine and mix the flour, baking powder, cinnamon, baking soda, and salt. In a medium bowl, combine and mix the bran cereal, carrot, milk, pineapple, and yogurt. Leave alone in bowl for 5 minutes. Combine and whisk the egg and honey into the medium bowl with the rest of its ingredients. Pour over dry the ingredients.

Spread into prepared pan. Smooth the top. Bake for about 30 minutes. Cool in pan. Use the foil overhang as handles and remove from pan.

Cut into bars.

Italian Apricot and Toasted Almond Cake

Serves 8

1½ cups all-purpose flour

¾ cup sugar

2 Tbsp sugar

1 Tbsp baking powder

Pinch salt

½ cup Ricotta cheese, part skim

2 Tbsp cold unsalted butter, cut into pieces

2 egg whites

2½ tsp water

2½ lbs ripe apricots, halved, pitted and cut into ½ inch wedges

3 Tbsp almonds, slivered

To make the dough, add the flour, ¾ cup of the sugar, the baking powder, and salt in a food processor. Pulse. Add the ricotta, butter, 1 egg white, and the water to the food processor. Pulse. The dough will come together. Take the dough out of the food processor. Shape it into a disk and wrap in plastic wrap. Refrigerate at least 1 hour to 24 hours.

Preheat the oven to 350 degrees Fahrenheit. Lightly spray a baking sheet with nonstick spray.

Place the refrigerated dough on the prepared baking sheet. Fold the edge of the dough over the baking sheet to form a ½ inch rim. Bake for 10 minutes. Cool on a wire rack for about 5 minutes.

Lightly beat the remaining egg white and brush it over the crust. Arrange the apricots on the crust in circles and sprinkle with the remaining 2 tablespoons sugar and the almonds. Bake for 20 minutes. The crust should be golden and the apricots should be soft.

Cool slightly on a wire rack.

Cut into 8 wedges. Serve warm or at room temperature.

Mixed Nuts

Makes 2 to 3 cups

3 cups mixed whole nuts (almonds, pecans, hazelnuts)

2 Tbsp safflower oil

2 tsp chili powder

¼ tsp cayenne pepper

½ tsp garlic powder

1 Tbsp sugar

½ tsp salt

Preheat oven to 300 degrees Fahrenheit.

Place the mixed nuts in a large bowl.

Heat the safflower oil in a heavy small saucepan over medium heat. Add the chili powder, garlic powder, and cayenne pepper. Stir for 15 seconds. Pour over the mixed nuts. Add the sugar and salt. Stir. Transfer to a baking pan.

Bake for 25 minutes. Nuts should be toasted.

Serve warm or at room temperature.

Cover and store at room temperature.

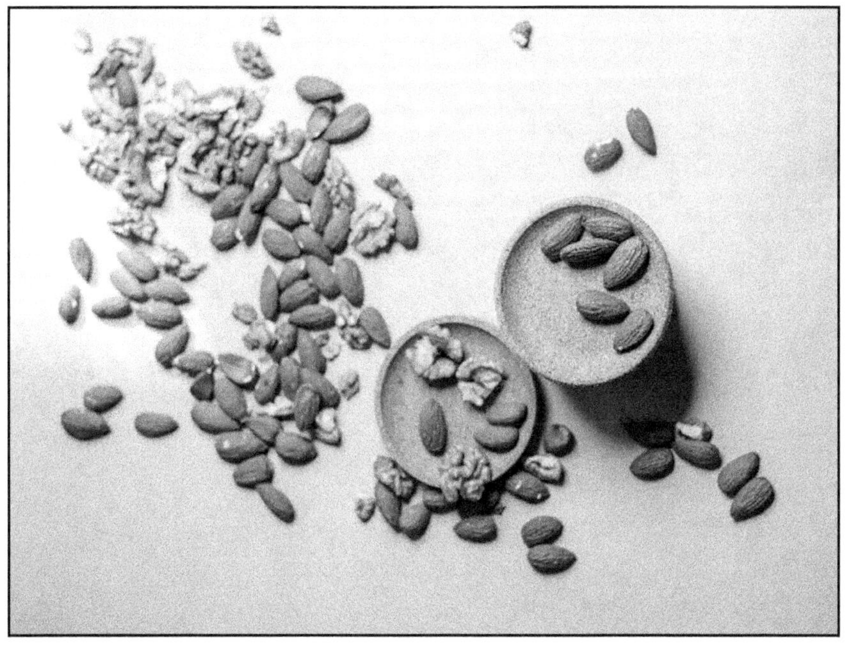

Cancer (June 21 to July 22)

The Moon rules Cancer. It governs emotions and instincts and is representative of the female principle.

The symbol for Cancer is the Crab. The crab has a hard-outer shell that shields soft flesh underneath.

The colors associated with Cancer are palc blue and silver. These are the colors of water and the moon.

Cancer is a cardinal water sign. Cardinal signs are visionaries. Water signs are emotional, intuitive, and have innate psychic abilities. Cancer people are motivated by activities that satisfy their emotional needs.

Cancer is a negative feminine sign.

Cancer rules the breasts, stomach, and fertility. These parts of the body symbolize nourishment and motherhood.

People born under the sign of Cancer are not easy to understand. They are unpredictable. They are like the tides of the oceans that shift to the effects of the moon. Cancerians are kind-hearted, generous, sympathetic, romantic, and imaginative on the positive side. They express their creativity through art, music, and writing. On the negative side, they can be too sensitive, moody, and downright "crabby." They can also be overly imaginative and prone to fantasy.

Cancer people have round-shaped bodies and are often said to have moon faces. Their height is small to average, and they can be stout. They have delicate features that make them appear gentle and kind. However, like the crab, they can have a tough exterior to drive them forward in life.

Cancer represents creativity, emotions, sensitivity, and nurturing. The dominant keywords for Cancerians are "I FEEL." Their dominant trait is loyalty. Some famous people born under the sign of Cancer are Diana, Princess of Wales, Harrison Ford, John Glenn, Tom Hanks, Ernest Hemingway, Rose Kennedy, Ann Landers, Nelson Mandela, Marshall McLuhan, Prince William, Sylvester Stallone, Ringo Starr, Meryl Streep, Robin Williams, and Andrew Wyeth.

Cancer people represent family and home. Food is a serious matter to them. Some of the world's best chefs are people who are born under the sun sign of Cancer. Cancer people are often overweight because they can easily retreat into their shells and seek food as solace when emotionally hurt. Cancerians love fatty foods and spicy spices to make them feel better when they feel low. They are also overweight because they do not like to do physical exercise. Cancerians are more sedentary than Taurus. Cancer people need to watch their diets to keep their weight under control. Fresh vegetables, fresh fruits, and lean proteins are crucial for Cancerians.

Being a water sign, Cancerians can eat fish and all types of seafood. They can also eat poultry and lean meats. Hearty soups and casseroles provide comfort food for the homebody Cancer.

People born under the sign of Cancer are sensitive. It is easy for them to get emotional and stressed out. Their tension and anxiety can lead to digestive disorders since Cancer rules the stomach. Cancerians are prone to ulcers, gall bladder upsets, and gastritis.

Cancer people need to eat foods that can assimilate easily to lessen the strain on the digestive system. Eating brown rice, baked potatoes with the skin on, and dried apricots can ease digestion.

One of the best foods Cancers can eat is cabbage because it is very therapeutic for the stomach. Cabbage also aids in weight loss because it is so low in calories. Cucumbers, watercress, and melons are also good foods that help digestion and weight loss.

Cancer people do very well when eating parsnips, white beets, avocados, bananas, and strawberries. These foods are high in fiber, keeping the digestive system in good working order. Pineapples and mangos are excellent choices for Cancers. Pineapples improve digestion, and mangos can make the stomach alkaline. More healthy food choices for Cancers are mushrooms and endive. They are low in sodium and calories and can keep Cancer's weight under control. Olives are very beneficial to Cancer people. They not only protect against ulcers, but they can prevent breast cancer.

It is not surprising that water plays a significant role in a Cancer's life. They can get dehydrated rather quickly, so they need plenty of liquids and eat tomatoes, oranges, and watermelons because these foods contain lots of water. Too much water in a Cancer's system can slow down their digestion and cause gain weight. Whole-grain cereals and dairy products are safe water regulating foods.

The mineral associated with Cancer is calcium fluoride. It helps keep elastic and connective tissues healthy in the body. Calcium fluoride is found in tooth enamel, fingernails, bones, and the eyes' lens. Varicose veins, receding gums, the curvature of the spine, and eye problems can occur if one has a deficiency of calcium fluoride. Oysters, egg yolks, yogurt, cheese, milk, rye, beets, broccoli, and cauliflower are food sources that contain calcium fluoride.

Skin disorders are common for Cancerians when there is a lack of calcium in their diet. Milk, cheese, and kale are good sources of calcium for Cancers. Okra, also high in calcium, aids in reducing stomach inflammation.

Even though Cancers are excellent cooks, they tend to use too much strong seasoning and should be reminded to hold the salt. Salt is not suitable for the Cancerian diet because it causes too much bloating. Most likely, Cancers will eat spicy and highly seasoned foods, but they need to use moderation because of their sensitive digestive tract. Cardamom, cumin, basil, garlic, mint, nutmeg, sage, and vanilla are some herbs and spices that Cancers can use.

Delicious, decadent desserts, ice cream, and chocolates are considered lunar foods. Being true moon children, Cancer people crave these foods. They need to be careful because an excess of sugar is not suitable for the stomach. They should eat fresh fruit and ice cream with low-fat whipped cream. White cake made with natural ingredients is allowed occasionally.

Water and fresh fruit juices are good drinks for Cancers. They both regulate the body's water. The stimulation from coffees and teas can increase Cancer people's slow metabolism. Cancers can drink a little vermouth, but they need to be careful with alcohol because of their over-indulgent nature.

Cancerians like to eat their meals with family in pleasant surroundings.

Cancer Food Guide

Fish

Anchovy
Bass
Bluefish
Carp
Catfish
Cod
Flounder
Grouper
Haddock
Halibut
Herring
Mackerel
Mahi-mahi
Monkfish
Ocean Perch
Orange Roughy
Red Snapper
Sablefish
Salmon
Sardine
Sea Bass
Shark
Smelt
Snapper
Sole
Sturgeon
Swordfish
Trout
Tuna
Turbot
Whitefish
Yellowtail

Seafood

Caviar
Clams
Crab
Crayfish
Lobster
Mussels
Octopus
Oysters
Scallops
Shrimp
Squid

Meat

Lean Red Meats
Veal
Venison

Poultry

Capon
Chicken
Cornish Game Hen
Duck
Goose
Pheasant
Quail
Turkey

Beans (High Carbohydrates)

Black-eyed Peas
Cannellini Beans
Chickpeas
Fava Beans
Garbanzo Beans
Great Northern Beans
Green Peas
Kidney
Lentils
Lima Beans
Navy Beans
Pinto Beans
Red Beans
Split Peas
White Beans

Grains/Breads/Cereals/Pastas

Amaranth
Barley
Bran
Brown Rice
Buckwheat
Kamut
Millet
Oats
Pumpernickel
Rye
Spelt
Tabbouleh
Wheat
Whole-Grain Foods

Cheese/Dairy Products

Butter
Cheeses (low fat)
Cream (low fat)
Eggs
Milk (low fat)
Sour Cream (low fat)
Yogurt (low fat)

Oils

Flax Seed Oil
Fish Oil
Olive Oil
Sesame Oil
Vegetable Oil

Vegetables

Alfalfa Sprouts
Artichokes
Arugula
Asparagus
Bean Sprouts
Beets
Beet Greens
Broccoli
Brussels Sprouts
Cabbage
Cauliflower
Carrots
Celery
Collard Greens
Cucumbers
Dandelion Greens
Eggplant
Endive
Green Beans
Hops
Kale
Leeks
Lettuces
Mushrooms
Mustard Greens
Okra
Onions
Parsnip
Peppers
Potatoes
Pumpkin
Radish
Spinach
Squash
Swiss Chard
Turnip
Turnip Greens
Watercress
Wax Beans
White Beets
Yellow Beans
Zucchini

Fruit

Apples
Apricots
Avocados
Bananas
Blackberries
Blueberries
Boysenberries
Coconut
Cranberries
Dried apricots
Grapefruit
Lemon
Lime
Mangos
Melons
Nectarines
Olives
Oranges
Peaches
Pears
Pineapple
Plums
Pomegranate
Prunes
Raisins
Raspberries
Strawberries
Tangerines
Tomatoes

Herbs and spices

Basil
Coriander
Nutmeg

Caraway
Cardamom
Capers
Cinnamon
Cilantro
Citron
Coriander
Citron
Coriander
Cumin
Citron
Cumin
Dill
Garlic
Ginger
Horseradish
Licorice
Marjoram
Mint
Mustard
Oregano
Parsley
Rosemary
Sage
Saffron
Sage
Sorrel
Tarragon
Thyme
Vanilla

Beverages

Coffee
Tea
Fresh Fruit Juices
Vermouth
Water

Cancer Food Recipes

Cancerians will fall in love with these recipes since food is the way to a Cancer's heart. Cancerians have a reputation for being excellent cooks. They prefer hearty homemade foods that often include recipes passed down from their grandmother.

Greek Spinach Frittata

Serves 4

1 16-oz container low fat or nonfat Cottage cheese
4 oz Feta cheese, crumbled
2 Tbsp flour
4 eggs

3 10-oz packages frozen spinach, thawed and well-drained
½ cup onion, minced
2 Tbsp lemon juice
2 Tbsp dried dill
Black pepper to taste
Lemon wedges for garnish

Preheat oven to 350 degrees Fahrenheit.

Spray a 9-inch round or square baking dish with nonstick cooking spray.

Add the nonfat Cottage cheese, Feta cheese, and flour to a food processor. Blend until smooth. Add the egg whites, drained spinach, onion, lemon juice, dill, and pepper. Mix well.

Pour the mixture into the prepared baking dish. Cook for 45 minutes. Cool 10 minutes before cutting.

Garnish with lemon wedges when serving.

Flank Steak

Serves 6

1½ lbs flank steak

1 red onion, quartered

½ cup capers, drained

2 Tbsp fresh oregano, chopped

4 cloves garlic, minced

¼ tsp salt

¼ tsp coarsely ground black pepper

Sliver one quarter of the onion and set aside. Chop the rest of the onion. In a bowl, add the chopped onion, capers, oregano, and garlic. Combine ¼ of this mixture with the slivered onions and set aside. Reserve the rest of the mixture.

Sprinkle both sides of the steak with salt and pepper. In a large zip-lock bag, combine the steak with the onion mixture. Marinate for at least 1 hour to 24 hours.

Heat the broiler. Remove the meat from the marinade. Discard the marinade. Place the meat on the broiler 4 inches from the heat. Broil the meat for 4 minutes on each side for medium-rare. Broil longer for medium or well-done.

Let the meat stand for 5 minutes before slicing. This will ensure that the juices stay inside the meat.

Place the meat on a platter. Pour the reserved onion mixture over the steak.

Orange and Pineapple Chicken Breasts

Serves 4 to 6

4 to 6 chicken breast halves

Salt and pepper

2 Tbsp vegetable oil

1 small can (6 oz) frozen orange juice concentrate, thawed

¾ cup melted margarine

1 tsp ground ginger

1½ tsp soy sauce

Pineapple slices

Preheat oven to 350 degrees Fahrenheit.

Place the vegetable oil in a shallow baking dish.

Season the chicken with salt and pepper. Add the chicken breast halves to the prepared baking dish.

Bake for 30 minutes.

Combine and mix the orange juice concentrate, margarine, ginger, and soy sauce. Simmer for 4 minutes. Baste the chicken with the sauce. Bake for an additional 35 minutes. Baste several times with the sauce. Place the chicken under the broiler until it is browned. This should take a few minutes.

Garnish with pineapple slices and serve over rice.

Maryland Crab Cakes

Makes 6

1 lb backfin Blue crab meat or other lump crab meat

9 saltine crackers

1 egg beaten

2 Tbsp mayonnaise

1 tsp mustard

½ tsp Worcestershire sauce

¼ tsp Old Bay seasoning

Salt to taste

2 Tbsp vegetable oil

Discard any cartilage from the crab meat. Put the crab meat in a bowl and set it aside.

Crush the saltine crackers and combine with all the other ingredients. Mix. Add enough crab meat only to combine with the other ingredients. Do not break up the crab meat into fine shreds. Shape the mixture into 6 crab cakes. Refrigerate for at least 1 hour.

Heat the vegetable oil in a nonstick frying pan. Add the crab cakes and cook for 4 minutes on each side. Crab cakes should be baked until golden brown.

Garnish with tartar sauce or with a squeeze of lemon before serving.

Salmon au Poivre with Watercress

Serves 4

4 skinless salmon fillets

1 Tbsp mixed peppercorns, coarsely crushed

¾ tsp salt

4 bunches watercress

½ red onion, thinly sliced

1½ tsp lemon juice

Olive oil nonstick spray

2½ tsp sesame seeds, toasted (optional)

Sprinkle the salmon with ½ teaspoon of the salt and with the peppercorns.

Spray a large nonstick skillet with nonstick spray. Place over medium-high heat. Add the salmon and cook for 4 minutes. Salmon should be lightly browned and opaque in the center.

In a large bowl, add the watercress, onion, lemon juice, sesame seeds, if using, and the remaining salt. Toss. Lightly spray with olive oil nonstick spray. Toss again.

Divide the watercress salad evenly among 4 plates. Top each serving with a piece of salmon.

Shrimp Newburg

Serves 6 to 8

3 Tbsp margarine

¾ lb fresh mushrooms, sliced

1 small onion minced

1 carrot grated

1½ cups half and half or low-fat half and half

1 Tbsp flour

1 cube seafood or chicken bouillon

3 lbs shrimp, cleaned and deveined

¼ tsp pepper

5 Tbsp Parmesan cheese, grated

Heat oven to 350 degrees Fahrenheit.

Melt margarine in saucepan. Add mushrooms, carrot, and onion. Cook for 5 minutes. Mushrooms should be golden brown. Place in a 4-quart casserole dish.

In a large bowl, combine and whisk the bouillon, flour, and half and half. Add shrimp, salt, and pepper. Stir. Place in casserole dish. Sprinkle with cheese.

Bake for 30 minutes. The shrimp should be pink and firm.

Serve over rice.

Tangy Tuna Steaks

Serves 4

2 tsp canola oil

2½ tsp reduced-sodium soy sauce

4 tuna steaks

1 Tbsp red-wine vinegar

2½ tsp flaxseed oil

2 tsp fresh ginger, peeled and minced

½ tsp salt

1 avocado, halved, pitted, peeled, and diced

1 11-oz can unsweetened mandarin orange sections, drained

½ red onion, chopped

Spray the broiler rack with nonstick spray.

Preheat the broiler.

In a small bowl, combine and whisk the canola oil and soy sauce. Brush the mixture on both sides of the tuna.

Place the tuna steaks on the broiler rack. Broil 5 inches from the heat for 3 minutes on each side for medium-done.

In a medium bowl, combine and whisk the vinegar, flaxseed oil, ginger, and salt. Add the avocado, mandarin orange sections, and onion. Toss to coat. Serve with the tuna.

Chicken Gumbo with Okra

Serves 4

1 Tbsp olive oil

3 onions, thinly sliced

4 skinless, boneless chicken thighs, trimmed and cut into chunks

3½ cups fresh or thawed frozen okra

1 14.5-oz can diced tomatoes

6 celery stalks with leaves, sliced

4 cloves garlic, peeled

2 cups reduced-sodium chicken broth

1½ tsp thyme

½ tsp salt

¼ tsp cayenne

2 tsp gumbo file powder

2 cups brown rice

Heat the oil in a nonstick skillet over medium-high heat. Add the onions and cook for 5 minutes. Onions should be soft.

Transfer the onions to a 5 or 6-quart slow cooker. Add the chicken, okra, tomatoes, celery, and garlic.

In a large glass bowl, add the broth, thyme, salt, and cayenne. Add to the slow cooker. Cover and cook for 4 to 6 hours on high or 8 to 10 hours on low. Chicken should be fork-tender.

Turn off the slow cooker. Discard the garlic. Stir in the gumbo file powder. Cover and let stand for 10 minutes. Flavors should be blended.

Cook the rice according to package directions.

Divide the rice evenly among 4 bowls and top with the gumbo.

Country Cabbage Soup

Serves 4

1 Tbsp extra-virgin olive oil

Pinch of salt

½ lb potatoes, skin on, cut ¼ inch pieces

4 cloves garlic, chopped

½ large yellow onion, thinly sliced

5 cups chicken or beef broth

1½ cups white beans, precooked or canned (drained & rinsed well)

1 medium cabbage, cored and sliced into ¼ inch ribbons

More extra-virgin olive oil for drizzling

¾ cup Parmesan cheese, freshly grated

Warm the olive oil in a large thick-bottomed pot over medium-high heat. Stir in the salt and potatoes. Cover and cook for 5 minutes. Potatoes should be tender and a little brown. Stir in the garlic and onion. Cook for 2 minutes. Add the chicken or beef broth and the beans. Simmer. Stir in the cabbage. Cook for 2 to 3 minutes. Cabbage should be softened.

Serve with a generous dusting of cheese.

Island Seafood Stew

Serves 6

3 white potatoes (Yukon gold preferred), peeled and cut into 1-inch chunks

1 onion, chopped

1 red bell pepper, coarsely chopped

4 cloves garlic, minced

3 14.5-oz cans diced tomatoes

1 bottle clam broth (8 oz)

½ tsp salt

¼ tsp salt

1 lb skinless halibut or cod fillets, cut into 1-inch pieces

¾ lb shrimp, peeled and deveined

2½ dozen littleneck clams, scrubbed

¾ cup shredded sweetened coconut, toasted

Grated zest of 1 lime

In a 5 or 6-quart slow cooker, add the potatoes, onions, bell pepper, garlic, and tomatoes and clam broth. Sprinkle with the salt and cayenne. Cover and cook for 4 to 5 hours on high or 8 to 10 hours on low. Potatoes should be fork-tender.

Add the halibut and shrimp to the slow cooker. Cover and cook for 10 minutes. Add the clams. Cover and cook until the halibut and shrimp are opaque and the clams open. Discard unopened clams.

Turn off the slow cooker. Let the stew stand for 5 minutes.

Ladle the stew evenly into 6 soup bowls. Sprinkle with the coconut and lime zest before serving.

Lobster Bisque with Sour Creme and Parsley

Serves 4

1 lobster (about 3 lbs)

1 medium onion

2 celery ribs

2 carrots

1 vine-ripened tomato

3 cloves garlic

2 Tbsp olive oil

2 Tbsp fresh tarragon leaves, chopped

2 Tbsp fresh thyme leaves, chopped

1 bay leaf

8 black peppercorns

¾ cup brandy

¾ cup dry Sherry

4 cups fish stock (available at fish stores and some specialty shops)

½ cup tomato paste

¾ cup low fat cream

1 Tbsp cornstarch

Salt

Pepper

Sour Cream

Parsley

Fill a 6-quart kettle three-fourths full of water. Add salt. Bring to a boil. Put the lobster headfirst into water. Cover and cook over high heat for 8 minutes. Transfer the lobster to a large bowl. Reserve 2 cups of the cooking liquid in a measuring cup.

After the lobster has cooled, twist off its tail and claws. Reserve the juices. Discard the head sacs and roe. Remove the meat from the claws and tail. Reserve the liver, shells, and body. The lobster meat will not be cooked through. Chop the lobster meat. Transfer to a bowl. Cover and chill.

Chop the onion, celery, carrot, tomato, and garlic. In a 6-quart heavy kettle, heat the olive oil over moderately high heat until hot. Sauté the reserved lobster shells and body for 8 minutes. Stir occasionally. Add the vegetables, garlic, herbs, peppercorns, brandy, and sherry. Simmer and stir for 5 minutes. Most of the liquid should be evaporated. Add the fish stock and reserved liver and reserved cooking liquid. Simmer the mixture uncovered for 1 hour. Stir occasionally. Reserve 2 tablespoons for the cornstarch.

Pour the mixture through a sieve into a large saucepan. Discard the solids. Add the tomato paste. Simmer for 10 minutes. Add the cream. Simmer for 5 minutes.

In a small bowl, combine the cornstarch and cooking liquid. Add to the bisque. Stir. Simmer and stir for 2 minutes. The bisque will thicken slightly. Add the lobster meat with any reserved juices. Simmer for 1 minute. The lobster meat should be cooked through.

Season the bisque with salt and pepper. Top with sour cream and parsley.

Leeks au Gratin Casserole

Serves 4

2 lbs leeks with tops cut into ½ inch pieces

1 Tbsp margarine

1 Tbsp all-purpose flour

½ tsp salt

Dash of pepper

¾ cup skim milk

¾ cup Gruyere cheese, shredded

2 Tbsp dry bread crumbs

1 tsp margarine

Preheat the oven to 325 degrees Fahrenheit.

Spray a shallow 1-quart casserole dish with nonstick cooking spray.

In a saucepan, add 1 inch of water and bring to a boil. Add the leeks. Cover and cook over medium heat for 5 minutes. The leeks should be crisp. Drain.

Melt 1 tablespoon margarine in a 2-quart saucepan over low heat. Add the flour, salt, and pepper. Cook over low heat for 2 to 3 minutes. Remove from heat. Stir in the milk gradually. Heat to boiling and stir for 1 minute. Stir in the cheese until it melts. Stir in the leeks. Pour into the prepared casserole dish.

To make a crumb topping, melt the 1 teaspoon of margarine in a small saucepan. In a small bowl, add the margarine and the bread crumbs to a small bowl. Mix. Pour over the leek mixture in the casserole dish.

Bake uncovered for 25 minutes.

Crab Salad Stuffed in Tomatoes

Serves 2

½ cup orzo

2 large tomatoes

1½ cup crabmeat

2 Tbsp reduced-fat Feta or Goat cheese, crumbles

2 Tbsp fresh dill, chopped

2 tsp balsamic vinegar

¼ tsp salt

¼ tsp pepper

½ cup black or green olives, optional

Cook the orzo according to package directions. Drain. Rinse under cold water. Drain again.

Cut a thin slice off the tops of the tomatoes. Reserve the tops. Scoop out the seeds and pulp with a spoon. Discard.

In a medium bowl, combine and toss the remaining ingredients and olives, if using. Spoon the crabmeat mixture evenly into the tomato shells and cover with the reserved tomato tops.

Angel Food Cake

Serves 8

1 cup cake flour

½ tsp salt

12 large egg whites at room temperature

1½ tsp cream of tartar

1½ cups sugar

2½ tsp vanilla extract

Preheat oven to 350 degrees Fahrenheit.

In a medium bowl, sift the flour and salt. Set aside.

Beat the egg whites with a mixer on medium-high heat for 1 minute. Eggs should be foamy. Add cream of tartar. Add the sugar and beat for 2 minutes. Stiff peaks should be formed. Add the vanilla. Transfer the mixture to a large, wide bowl.

Sift the flour and salt mixture over the egg-white mixture. Stir to combine all the ingredients very well.

Spoon the batter into an ungreased angel-food cake pan with a removable bottom.

Release air bubbles in the batter by running a small spatula through the batter.

Bake for 35 minutes. Cake should spring back when lightly pressed.

Invert the cake pan. Let the cake cool in the pan for 1 hour.

Run a knife around the inside of the pan and around the tube to release. Also, use the knife to release the cake from the bottom of the pan and remove.

Top the cake with strawberries, blueberries, raspberries, and whipped cream before serving.

Fresh Fruit with Mint

Serves 4 to 6

1 medium watermelon
1 small cantaloupe
1 small honeydew
2½ cups pineapple chunks, fresh or canned
2½ strawberry halves
Mint sprigs, for garnish

Scoop the watermelon, cantaloupe, and honeydew melons with a melon baller. Remove seeds from the melons. Cover and chill.

Combine the rest of fruit in a bowl. Chill.

Spoon fruit into one bowl and garnish with mint before serving.

Leo (July 23 to August 22)

The sun rules Leo. The sun radiates heat and energy, and it gives us light and generates vitality.

The symbol associated with Leo is the lion. The lion is brave and strong, and it possesses nobility and pride because it is the jungle king.

The colors associated with Leo are gold and orange.

Leo is a fixed fire sign. Fixed signs are persistent and can withstand tremendous pressure. Fire signs are energetic, assertive, and dynamic. Leos are high-spirited, determined individuals who have great perseverance.

Leo is a positive masculine sign.

Leo rules the heart, spine, and back. The heart is associated with love, and the back is associated with courage.

Leos are highly energetic, positive, and optimistic people. They are magnetic, charming, and alluring, passionate, and affectionate. Leos are probably the most charismatic and extroverted people out of all the zodiac personalities. Leos can be stylish, and they have their own way of doing things.

Like the lion, Leos are courageous, ambitious, dominant, strong-willed, independent, self-confident, and fun-loving. They are born leaders. They are dignified, vigorous, and wise. Leos live a life of luxury because they think they are the monarch of the human race.

Leos are very healthy. They are known to live a very long time. They have strong constitutions and proper coordination. They have flexible spines. They are physically active, and they have well-built physiques. They have broad shoulders and good muscle tone. They are athletically inclined and excellent dancers.

Leo represents creativity and authority. The dominant keywords for Leos are "I WILL." Their dominant trait is exuberance. Some famous people born under the sign of Leo are Paul Anka, Neil Armstrong, Lucille Ball, Bill Clinton, Robert DeNiro, Amelia Earhart, Dustin Hoffman, Mick Jagger, Magic Johnson, Madonna, Barack Obama, Jacqueline Kennedy Onassis, Robert Redford, Arnold Schwarzenegger, and Andy Warhol.

Leos love food. Eating well is part of the Leo tradition. Like a king, they like to sit down to a feast. Fortunately, they have a high metabolism, strong stomachs, and good circulation for all the rich food and fine wine they like to intake.

Leos love all types of food. They like bread and pasta with red tomato sauce, T-bone steak, and a roast with trimmings. They like hot soups. Leos like exotic dishes such as caviar, turbot, and wild game with wine sauce. They like rich and robust dishes like coconut curries.

Leos can suffer from overexertion because they push themselves too much. Their upper back can tire quickly. Leos should eat high protein foods like fish, seafood, lean meat, poultry, eggs, and cheese to fuel their busy lifestyles. Leos also need to eat foods high in carbohydrates so their bodies can receive and sustain energy. Apples, figs, lemons, honey, and peaches are some of the foods in this category. Other foods known to maintain energy in the body are tomatoes, eggplant, peppers, pineapples, and mandarins. Leos should drink goat's milk because it is rich in whey protein and will keep them physically healthy.

Leos can also suffer from bad nerves because they push themselves too much. Bananas, carrots, celery, coconut, prunes, and wheat germ are good foods to eat because they support the nervous system. Plums, pears, and oranges can reduce heart strain sometimes caused by nervousness. Dried fruit and mineral water are good to consume because they provide the body with essential minerals such as calcium, zinc, magnesium, and phosphate that can get depleted when bad nerves cause stress.

Leos should consider following a Mediterranean-style diet because it is rich in olive oil, which is good for the heart, and this diet is regarded as one of the best in the world.

Leos should stay away from foods high in saturated fats. They should eat foods that contain Omega-3, a polyunsaturated fatty acid. Omega-3 foods prevent heart disease. They lower cholesterol and triglycerides levels which cause strokes and heart attacks. Fish and seafood that contain Omega-3 are anchovies, oysters, salmon, sardine, tuna, and whitefish. Oatmeal, beans, Brussels sprouts, onions, watercress, avocados, berries, and flaxseed oil are other examples of foods that have Omega-3.

Leos need to have iron in their diet because it benefits the heart. Red meat, liver, artichokes, collards, kale, spinach, raisins, and dates are some foods that are rich in iron.

Grapes are good for Leos to eat. They keep the heart muscles healthy.

The mineral associated with Leo is magnesium phosphate. It aids in the formation of the skeletal structure and maintains the fluidity of the blood. It also supports muscle cells and nerves and activates digestive enzymes. Foods that contain this mineral are whole wheat and rye products, almonds, walnuts, sunflower seeds, rice, seafood, beets, asparagus, romaine lettuce, and egg yolk. Foods that aid blood circulation and have blood-making properties are beef, lamb, poultry, fresh fruit, salad greens, cheese, whole milk, and yogurt.

Spices are important to Leos because of their love of food. Leos love to taste their food. However, they need to be careful of spicy and highly seasoned foods because of their propensity towards heartburn. Like Cancers, they need to use certain spices and herbs in moderation. Basil, fennel, and parsley can lower cholesterol and blood pressure. Rosemary can reduce blood pressure. Ginger is good for circulation and keeps the body warm. Other good herbs and spices for Leos include anise, clove, chicory, coriander, nutmeg, and tarragon. Leos love saffron, an expensive and colorful spice.

Leos find it very difficult to pass up desserts, and they like decadent chocolates to light and fluffy cheesecakes. Leos should try to stay away from desserts high in calories and fat. Lemon and orange cakes, as well as lemon cookies, can revitalize Leos. Leos can also try desserts made with coconut since it lowers cholesterol. Fresh fruit with whipped low fat whipped cream is the safest bet for Leos.

Leos can drink almost anything because of their strong constitution. They love their wine and enjoy their exotic coffees. Green tea is excellent for Leos to drink because it prevents heart disease and stroke by lowering cholesterol levels. It also prevents hypertension. Red wine also brings down cholesterol levels. Chamomile tea is good for Leos because it calms their nerves when they get stressed out.

Like royalty, Leos like to sit down to feasts. Much like the Taurus personality, Leos like company when they eat.

Leo Food Guide

Fish

Anchovy
Bass
Bluefish
Carp
Catfish
Cod
Flounder
Grouper
Haddock
Halibut
Herring
Mackerel
Mahi-mahi
Monkfish
Ocean Perch
Orange Roughy
Red Snapper
Sablefish
Salmon
Sardine
Sea Bass
Shark
Smelt
Snapper
Sole
Sturgeon
Swordfish
Trout
Tuna
Turbot
Whitefish
Yellowtail

Seafood

Caviar
Clams
Crab
Crayfish
Lobster
Mussels
Octopus
Oysters
Scallops
Shrimp
Squid

Meat

Bacon
Beef
Lamb
Liver
Pork
Sausage
Steak
Veal
Venison

Poultry

Capon
Chicken
Cornish Game Hen
Duck
Goose
Pheasant
Quail
Turkey

Beans (High Carbohydrates)

Black-eyed Peas
Cannellini Beans
Chick Peas
Great Northern Beans
Green Peas
Kidney
Navy Beans
Pinto Beans
Red Beans

Fava Beans
Garbanzo Beans
Lentils
Lima Beans
Split Peas
White Beans

Grains/Breads/Cereals/Pastas

Amaranth
Barley
Bran
Brown Rice
Buckwheat
Kamut
Millet
Oats
Pumpernickel
Rye
Spelt
Wheat
Tabbouleh
Whole-Grain Foods

Cheese/Dairy Products

Butter
Cheeses
Cream
Eggs
Milk
Sour Cream
Yogurt

Oils

Flax Seed Oil
Fish Oil
Olive Oil
Sesame Oil
Vegetable Oil

Vegetables

Alfalfa Sprouts
Artichokes
Cucumbers
Dandelion Greens
Peppers
Potatoes

Arugula
Asparagus
Bean Sprouts
Beets
Beet Greens
Broccoli
Brussels Sprouts
Cabbage
Cauliflower
Carrots
Celery
Collard Greens
Eggplant
Endive
Green Beans
Hops
Kale
Leeks
Lettuces
Mushrooms
Mustard Greens
Okra
Onions
Parsnip
Pumpkin
Radish
Spinach
Squash
Swiss Chard
Turnip
Turnip Greens
Watercress
Wax Beans
White Beans
Yellow Beans
Zucchini

Fruit

Apples
Apricots
Avocados
Bananas
Blackberries
Blueberries
Boysenberries
Coconut
Cranberries
Dates
Dried fruit
Figs
Grapes
Grapefruit
Lemon
Lime
Mandarins
Mangos
Melons
Nectarines
Oranges
Peaches
Pear
Pineapple
Plum
Pomegranate
Prunes
Raisins
Raspberries
Strawberries
Tangerines

Herbs and Spices

Anise
Basil
Capers
Caraway
Cardamom
Chicory
Cilantro
Cinnamon
Clove
Oregano
Cumin
Dill
Fennel
Garlic
Ginger
Lemon balm
Marjoram
Mint
Nutmeg
Parsley
Rosemary
Saffron
Sage
Sesame
Tarragon
Thyme
Turmeric
Coriander

Beverages

Coffee
Herbal teas
Mineral Water
Red Wine
White wine

Other

Almonds
Honey
Pumpkin Seeds
Sunflower Seeds
Walnuts

Leo Food Recipes

Leos have a luxurious palate, preferring expensive foods prepared with high-quality ingredients. If their budget affords, they will happily feast on royal delights such as lobsters, oysters, and caviar.

Mint Lamb Chops

Serves 4

¼ cup olive oil

½ cup fresh mint, chopped

3 cloves garlic, minced

1½ tsp salt

2 tsp cumin, ground

1 tsp coriander, ground

½ tsp cayenne pepper

1 tsp freshly ground black pepper

8 lamb loin chops (1 to 1½ inch thick, about 5 oz), trimmed

Fresh mint sprigs, for garnish

In a small bowl, add and mix the olive, mint, minced garlic, salt, cumin, coriander, cayenne pepper, and black pepper. Spread over both sides of the lamb chops. Let the chops sit for 10 minutes. Transfer chops to broiler pan and let them sit for 10 minutes.

Preheat the broiler.

Transfer the chops to the broiler. Broil for 4 minutes for medium-rare. The chops should be brown and crusty.

Arrange chops on platter.

Garnish with fresh mint sprigs and serve.

Tuscany T-bone Steak with Chianti Butter

Serves 2 to 3

1 porterhouse steak (about 2 ½ to 3 lbs), cut 2½ to 3 inches thick

2 Tbsp olive oil

1 Tbsp salt

1 tsp coarsely freshly ground black pepper

3 large onions cut into 1-inch chunks

4 oz arugula

1 stick of unsalted butter at room temperature

2 tsp Chianti or any medium-bodied red wine

½ tsp salt

For the Chianti butter, soften the butter in a mixing bowl. Add the wine and salt. Mix.

Place on a sheet of plastic wrap. Shape into a log and twist the ends to seal. Refrigerate to harden.

Preheat the oven to 500 degrees Fahrenheit. Position one oven rack in the top third of the oven and a second rack in the bottom of the oven.

Brush the steak with olive oil. Season with the salt and pepper. Let the steak sit uncovered, at room temperature, for 30 minutes.

Fill a 13 x 9-inch baking dish with enough onions to completely cover the bottom. Place the baking dish on the lower rack. Place the steak directly on the top rack. Position it above the dish in the oven. Turn the steak after 15 minutes. Roast for 35 minutes for medium-rare. Check periodically to make sure steak is not burning.

Chicken Masala

Serves 4

1 Tbsp olive oil

1 medium onion, finely chopped

2 Tbsp fresh garlic, finely chopped

2 Tbsp fresh ginger, finely chopped

1 tsp ground cumin

1½ tsp cayenne

1 Tbsp coriander seeds

1 Tbsp garam masala

½ paprika

1 tsp turmeric

1 tsp salt

1½ Tbsp tomato paste

1 lb chicken thighs, boneless

2½ cups tomatoes

2½ cups potatoes, chopped

14 cashew nuts

1 cup coconut milk

2½ cups water

½ cup loosely packed fresh cilantro leaves, for garnish

Heat the olive oil in a large saucepan over medium-high heat. Add the onion, garlic, ginger, cumin, and cayenne. Sauté for 3 minutes. The onions should be softened. Add the coriander seed, garam masala, paprika, turmeric, and salt. Toast for 10 seconds.

Add the tomato paste. Stir well. Add the chicken thighs. Cook for 5 minutes. Turn once. Add the tomatoes, potatoes, cashews, coconut milk, and water. Mix well. Bring to a boil. Reduce the heat. Simmer.

Cover and cook for 25 minutes. Chicken should be cooked through. Garnish with cilantro leaves.

Serve with rice.

Chicken Thighs with Artichoke Panzanella

Serves 4

8 bone-in, skin-on chicken thighs (about 3 lbs)
5 cloves garlic
1¼ inch piece of fresh ginger, peeled and coarsely chopped
2 tsp sweet paprika
½ tsp cayenne
½ cup plus 1 Tbsp fresh lemon juice
2 Tbsp chopped cilantro leaves
1 scallion, thinly sliced
½ cup extra-virgin olive oil
½ cup chopped flat-leaf parsley
1¾ lb loaf white country-style bread, sliced 1 inch thick
Salt
Freshly ground pepper
16 oz cherry tomatoes
8 baby artichokes in oil, drained and halved lengthwise
1 Tbsp grated lemon zest
1 Tbsp canola oil
½ cup chicken stock

Pulse the garlic and ginger in a small food processor. Add the paprika, cayenne, and ⅓ cup of the lemon juice. Process. Transfer to a bowl. Add and toss the chicken, cilantro, scallion, and 2 tablespoons of the olive oil, and 2 tablespoons of the parsley. Cover and refrigerate for at least 3 hours.

Heat a grill pan. Brush the bread with 3 tablespoons of the olive oil. Season with salt and pepper. Grill the bread over moderately high heat for 3 minutes. Turn once. Bread should be toasted. Tear the bread into small pieces once it has cooled down.

Preheat the broiler. Heat 1 tablespoon of the olive oil in a large, deep skillet. Add the tomatoes and season with salt and pepper. Broil the tomatoes for 7 minutes. Mash the tomatoes with a spoon to release some of their juices. Let the tomatoes cool. Add the bread, artichokes, and lemon zest to the skillet.

Preheat the oven to 375 degrees Fahrenheit.

Remove the chicken thighs from the marinade. Pat dry. Season with salt and pepper.

Heat the canola oil in a large skillet. Add the chicken to the skillet, skin side down. Cook over moderately high heat for 4 minutes. Chicken should be browned. Add the chicken stock to the skillet. Bring to a boil. Transfer the skillet to the oven. Roast the chicken for 15 minutes. Chicken should be cooked through. Spoon ¼ cup of the pan drippings from the skillet over the bread mixture.

In a small bowl, whisk the remaining 2 tablespoons of olive oil, 2 tablespoons of parsley and the remaining 1 tablespoon of lemon juice. Warm the bread mixture over moderate heat for 2 minutes. Remove from the heat. Pour the dressing over the bread salad. Toss. Season with salt and pepper.
Transfer the chicken to plates. Spoon the bread salad alongside and serve.

Greek Chicken Kabobs

Serves 2

1 8-oz container fat-free or low fat plain yogurt
½ cup crumbled Feta cheese with basil and sun-dried tomatoes
½ tsp lemon zest
2 Tbsp fresh lemon juice
2 tsp dried oregano
½ tsp salt
¼ tsp ground black pepper
½ tsp dried rosemary, crushed
1 lb skinless, boneless chicken breast halves – cut into 1-inch pieces
1 red onion, cut into wedges
1 large green bell pepper, cut into 1½ inch pieces

In a large shallow baking dish, add and mix the yogurt, Feta cheese, lemon zest, lemon juice, oregano, salt, pepper, and rosemary. Place the chicken in the dish. Coat. Cover and marinate in the refrigerator for 3 hours.

Preheat an outdoor grill for high heat. Can also preheat an oven grill.

Thread the chicken, onion wedges, and green bell pepper pieces alternately onto skewers. Discard the remaining yogurt mixture.

Grill the skewers on the prepared grill until the chicken is no longer pink and juices run clear.

Red Snapper

Serves 4

2 red snapper fillets, skinned and cut crosswise in half
1 15-oz can crushed tomatoes
½ tsp salt
½ tsp dried oregano
½ tsp black pepper
¼ cup crumbled Feta cheese

Preheat the oven to 350 degrees Fahrenheit.

In a small bowl, combine and stir the tomatoes, ¼ teaspoon of the salt, oregano, and ¼ teaspoon of the pepper.

Spread half of the tomato sauce in a 7 x 11-inch baking dish. Arrange the snapper on top of the sauce in one layer. Sprinkle the fish with the remaining salt and pepper. Spoon the remaining tomato sauce evenly over the fish and sprinkle with the Feta cheese.

Cover the dish tightly with foil. Bake the fish for 20 minutes. Fish should be opaque in the center.

Serve with couscous or rice.

Broiled Lobster Tails

Serves 4

4 lobster tails

1½ cups butter, melted

Salt

Ground white pepper

2 lemons, cut into wedges, for garnish

Preheat the broiler.

Place the lobster tails on a baking sheet. With a sharp knife or kitchen shears, carefully cut top side of lobster shells lengthwise. Pull apart shells slightly, and season meat with equal amounts butter, paprika, salt, and white pepper.

Broil the lobster tails for 7 to 10 minutes. Lobster tails should be lightly browned.

Garnish with lemon wedges and serve.

Lemon Black Cod with Swiss Chard and Olives

Serves 4

1 lemon, stem removed

¼ tsp coriander seeds

¼ tsp cumin seeds

2 Tbsp olive oil, divided

4 4-oz pieces skin-on black cod fillet

Salt

Freshly ground black pepper

2 garlic cloves, chopped

2 large bunches Swiss chard (about 1 ½ lbs total), ribs and stems removed, leaves torn

2 Tbsp cured black olives, pitted, sliced

Place the lemon in a small saucepan and add water just to cover. Place a small heatproof plate on top of the lemon inside the saucepan. This will keep the lemon submerged. Bring the water to a boil. Reduce heat. Simmer for 30 minutes. Lemon should be tender. Drain. Cut lemon in half and cool.

Scoop out the pulp from both the lemon halves and press pulp through a coarse-mesh sieve into a small bowl. Discard the solids. Finely chop and peel. Add to pulp. Set aside.

In a small skillet over medium heat, add and stir the coriander and cumin seeds for 3 minutes. Coriander and cumin seeds should be slightly darkened and fragrant. Coarsely grind the coriander and cumin seeds in a spice mill or with a mortar and pestle.

In a medium bowl, season the fish with the spice mixture. Add the salt and pepper. Heat 1 tablespoon of olive oil in a large nonstick skillet over medium-high heat. Place the fish skin down in the skillet. Cook for 5 minutes. Fish should be browned and crisp. Turn the fish and cook for 4 more minutes. Fish should be opaque in the middle.

Heat the remaining 1 tablespoon in oil in a large skillet over medium heat. Add the garlic. Cook for 30 seconds. Add the Swiss chard by the handful, tossing and allowing it to wilt slightly between additions. Season with salt and pepper. Cook for 7 minutes. Set aside.

Mix the olives and the reserved lemon mixture into the Swiss chard.

Serve the fish with the Swiss chard.

Leo Seafood Paella

Serves 4

1 large onion, finely chopped

6 Tbsp olive oil

2 garlic cloves, finely chopped

2 tomatoes, peeled and chopped

½ tsp sugar

Salt

1 tsp sweet paprika

Pinch of saffron threads

4 cleaned squids, bodies sliced into ¼ inch-wide rings, tentacles left whole

2 cups medium grain Spanish paella rice or risotto rice

3½ cups fish or chicken stock, plus more if needed

1½ cups dry wine

12 jumbo shrimp in their shells

16 mussels, scrubbed and debearded

12 jumbo shrimp in their shells

Add the olive oil to a 16-inch paella pan and fry the onion until it is soft. Stir often. Add the garlic. Stir and cook for 3 minutes. Add the tomatoes, sugar, paprika, saffron, and salt. Stir well. Cook until the tomatoes are reduced to a sauce and the oil is sizzling. Add the squid. Cook for 2 minutes. Add the rice. Stir until all the grains are coated.

Add the chicken or fish stock and wine to a saucepan. Bring to a boil. Pour over the rice. Bring to a boil. Add salt to taste. Stir well. Spread the rice out evenly in the pan. Cook the rice over low heat for 20 minutes. Move the pan around and rotate it so the rice cooks evenly. After 10 minutes of cooking, lay the shrimp on top and turn them when they become pink. Add a little more hot stock if the rice is too dry and if there are crackly frying noises. Turn off the heat when the rice is finished cooking. Cover the pan with a large piece of aluminum foil.

Steam the mussels with a very small amount of water in a pan with a tight-fitting lid. As soon as they open, they are cooked. Throw away any mussels that have not opened.

Arrange the mussels on top of the paella.

Seared Scallops with Leeks and Caviar Sauce

Serves 4

20 sea scallops

3 Tbsp butter

2 large leeks (white and pale green parts only), chopped

1 cup brut champagne

1 cup whipping cream

4 Tbsp

1¾ tsp fresh tarragon, chopped

Melt 2 tablespoons butter in a heavy large skillet over medium-low heat. Add the leeks and sauté for 20 minutes. Leeks should be tender. Add the champagne. Boil for 4 minutes. Liquid should be reduced to about ½ cup. Transfer the leek mixture to a strainer that is set over a bowl. Press on the leeks to extract as much liquid as possible. Transfer the leeks to a small bowl. Season with salt and pepper. Return the liquid to same skillet. Add the cream. Boil for 4 minutes. Liquid should be reduced to about ¾ cup. Transfer the sauce to a bowl. Cool for 1 hour. Add the caviar and the tarragon. Stir.

Melt 1 tablespoon butter in large nonstick skillet over medium heat. Season the scallops with salt and pepper. Add the scallops to the skillet in batches and sauté for about 3 minutes. Scallops should be cooked through and golden brown. Transfer to a plate.

Spoon the leeks in 5 small mounds around the rim of each plate using four plates. Equally space them. Top each mound with 1 scallop. Spoon the sauce into the center of each plate.

Spaghetti and Meatballs

Serves 6

4 Tbsp olive oil

1 cup onion, chopped

4 cloves garlic, minced

1 16-oz can crushed tomatoes

3 6-oz cans tomato paste

1 cup water

½ cup sugar

¼ cup fresh oregano, chopped and divided

¼ cup thyme

1 bay leaf

Salt

Pepper

1 lb ground hamburger

½ cup Italian seasoned bread crumbs

¼ cup fresh parsley, chopped

2 eggs lightly beaten

¾ cup grated Parmesan cheese

1 16-oz package uncooked spaghetti

Heat the olive oil in a large saucepan over medium heat. Cook the onion until it is lightly brown. Add 2 cloves of garlic. Cook for 1 minute. Add the crushed tomatoes, tomato paste, water, sugar, half of the oregano, thyme, and bay leaf. Season with salt and pepper. Bring to a boil. Reduce heat to low. Simmer.

For the meatballs, add the hamburger, bread crumbs, the remaining oregano, the remaining garlic, parsley, eggs, and cheese to a large bowl. Mix well. Season with salt and pepper. Roll into 1-inch balls and add to the sauce. Cook for 40 minutes.

Cook the spaghetti according to package directions. Serve the meatballs and sauce over the cooked spaghetti.

Asparagus and Hollandaise Sauce

Serves 4

6 Tbsp unsalted butter

2 large egg yolks, at room temperature

3 Tbsp freshly squeezed lemon juice

Salt

Freshly ground black pepper

Pinch of cayenne pepper

1 lb fresh asparagus

Olive Oil

Preheat the oven to 400 degrees Fahrenheit.

Melt the butter in a small saucepan. Place the egg yolks, lemon juice, salt, pepper, and cayenne in a blender. Blend for 15 seconds. Slowly pour the hot butter into the blender while it is running. Blend for 30 seconds. Sauce should be thick.

Break off the tough ends of the asparagus. Peel the asparagus if it is too thick. Place the asparagus on a baking sheet. Coat the asparagus with olive oil. Season with salt and pepper.

Roast the asparagus for 15 to 20 minutes. Asparagus should be tender and crisp

Pour the hollandaise sauce over the warm asparagus and serve.

Rosemary and Garlic Roasted Potatoes

Serves 2 to 3

1 lb of white or new potatoes

5 Tbsp olive oil

2 rosemary sprigs

6 cloves garlic, lightly smashed

Salt

Pepper

Heat the oven to 500 degrees Fahrenheit.

Clean the potatoes. Dry and quarter them.

Add the olive oil to a 3-quart baking dish. When the oven is heated, place the baking dish on the bottom rack. Heat the oil for 3 minutes. Oil should be hot and shimmering. Remove the dish from the oven. Add the potatoes, rosemary, and garlic. Stir to coat in the oil. Add salt and pepper.

Return the dish to the bottom rack of the oven. Roast the potatoes for 35 minutes. Potatoes should be a dark golden brown and have a nice crust.

Serve with lamb.

Italian Minestrone Soup

Serves 4

3½ cups vegetable or chicken broth
1 28-oz can diced tomatoes
1 15-oz can white (cannellini) beans, drained
4 carrots, peeled and chopped
2 celery stalks, chopped
1½ cups onion, chopped
1 tsp dried thyme
½ tsp dried sage
¼ tsp dried oregano
1 bay leaf
½ tsp salt
½ tsp black ground pepper
2 cups cooked tubular or spiral pasta
2 small zucchinis, chopped
2 cups coarsely chopped fresh or frozen spinach, defrosted
4 Tbsp grated Parmesan or Romano cheese
Basil sprigs for garnish, optional

In a slow cooker, add the broth, tomatoes, beans, carrots, celery, onion, thyme, sage, oregano, bay leaf, salt, and pepper. Cover and cook on low heat for 6 to 8 hours or on high heat for 3 to 4 hours.

Add the pasta, zucchini, and spinach 30 minutes before the soup is finished cooking. Cover and cook for an additional 30 minutes. Remove the bay leaf.

Ladle the soup into bowls. Sprinkle with Parmesan or Romano cheese. Garnish with basil, if desired. Serve.

Avocado and Spinach Salad with Oranges

Serves 8

½ cup fresh orange juice
¾ cup Sherry wine vinegar
3 Tbsp honey
1 Tbsp fresh lime juice
½ tsp chili powder
½ tsp salt
¼ tsp pepper
¾ cup olive oil
2 6-oz packages baby spinach
4 oranges, peeled, pith removed and quartered,
1 avocado, peeled, seeded cubed
¾ cup red onion, chopped
¼ cup fresh cilantro, chopped
Salt
Pepper

In a large bowl, add the orange juice, sherry wine vinegar, honey, lime juice, chili powder, salt, and pepper. Whisk. Gradually add the olive oil. Whisk.
In a second large bowl, add the remaining ingredients. Toss the salad with the dressing.

Lemon Lime Cake with Lime Whipped Cream

Makes 1 cake

1 cup sugar
¾ cup butter
2 eggs
1 tsp vanilla
2 Tbsp lime zest
2 Tbsp tablespoon lemon zest
1 ¾ cups flour
1 tsp baking powder
¼ cup milk
3 tablespoons lemon and/or lime juice
1-pint cold whipping cream
¼ tsp vanilla extract
1 Tbsp lime zest
3 Tbsp powdered sugar

Preheat the oven to 350 degrees Fahrenheit.

In a medium bowl, add the butter, sugar, and eggs. Cream together until fluffy. Add the vanilla and zest. Mix well.

In a second bowl, add the dry ingredients. Mix. Add the lemon or lime juice. Mix. Add the milk. Beat and mix until all the ingredients are thoroughly mixed.

Pour into an 8 x 8 or 9 x 9 square cake pan. Bake for 30 minutes. Cool completely.

For the lime whipped cream, add the cream, vanilla, sugar, and lime zest to a bowl of an electric mixer. Beat for about 5 minutes. The mixture should be stiff.

Frost cake. Serve and refrigerate.

Virgo (August 23 to September 22)

Like Gemini, Virgo is ruled by the planet Mercury. Mercury rules communication and commerce and governs intelligence and intellectual reasoning.

The symbol associated with Virgo is the Virgin, holding a cluster of wheat. The Virgin represents purity. The Virgin is reserved, modest, and shy. The Virgin represents the harvest because of the grain she is carrying.

The colors associated with Virgo are all shades of green.

Virgo is a mutable earth sign. Mutable signs are open to change. Earth signs are sensible. Virgos are open to new thoughts and ideas. They also know how to utilize new thoughts and ideas.

Virgo is a negative feminine sign.

Virgo rules the nervous system and the intestines. The intestines assimilate food into the body.

Like any other earth sign, Virgos are practical and down to earth. They are rational. They seek to know and to understand. Virgos have an unusual ability to reason because they are so logical in their thinking. Virgos are just as intelligent, quick-witted, and communicative as Geminis because Mercury rules both signs. Virgos, however, are more observant and reflective.

Virgos are industrious. They like to work, and they believe in self-improvement not only for themselves but also for others. They make the most out of any opportunity, using it to benefit themselves and others. Virgos can dig deep to gather information because they are detail-oriented and possess excellent analytical skills. They are clear thinkers, and they have good memories.

Virgos pride themselves on being organized, efficient, and productive. Often, they don't see how critical they are because they are perfectionists at heart. They are also highly intuitive and discriminating because of their finely tuned nervous system, making them compulsive and anxious.

Although Virgos can come across as unemotional and temperamental, we must remember what Virgo represents. The Virgin's representation of purity means "purity of purpose." Virgos have high motives. They want to help humanity. Symbolically, the Virgin's image of the harvest indicates one who gathers food and feeds and nourishes others. Virgos use their knowledge and skills to benefit or "feed" the world. Virgos love to be of service to others. They are humble, and they work quietly.

In appearance, Virgos are very well-groomed and elegant people. They have good taste in dress. They are average to tall with a slender build. Virgos are more intellectual than physical, so it is hard for them to exercise. However, they are one of the signs that are most unlikely to experience health problems since they are continuously improving themselves.

Virgo represents wisdom. The dominant keywords for Virgos are "I ANALYZE." Their dominant trait is conscientiousness. Some famous people born under the sign of Virgo are Kobe Bryant, Taylor Caldwell, Agatha Christie, Confucius, Sean Connery, Harry Connick Jr., Richard Gere, Hugh Grant, Michael Jackson, Tommy Lee Jones, Margaret Sanger, Charlie Sheen, Oliver Stone, Mother Teresa, and Lily Tomlin.

Virgos have a slow metabolism, but their strong belief in balance and moderation helps them fight against weight gain and careless eating patterns. Virgos are not food gourmets, but they are particular about the quality and variety of their food. They like low-fat foods like Japanese and French cuisines. Virgos gravitate towards healthy and natural foods. They enjoy eating salads with fresh vegetables, and they like fresh fruits. Many Virgos are vegetarians. They tend to eat the most fruits and vegetables of all the zodiac signs. It is not surprising since Virgo rules the autumn harvest.

Virgos are prone to digestive problems and intestinal infections. They can suffer from ulcers, liver upsets, colitis, bowel problems, and gas pains. Virgos usually do not eat fried foods or foods laden with heavy sauces and gravies, leading to such issues. They like boiled chicken and veal stew, which are suitable for them, and they tend to stay away from grilled meat and pork dishes. Virgos should eat brown rice, yogurt, eggs, and cottage cheese because these foods are easy to digest.

Virgos are prone to nervous tension, anxiety, and emotional stress because of their sensitive nervous systems. These problems are reflected in physical ailments because Mercury controls the link between the mind and the body. For example,

Virgos are the "worriers" of the zodiac, and when they worry too much, they develop ulcers. Virgos need to stay calm and relaxed for them to stay healthy. Lean red meats, halibut, shrimp, lobster, spinach, legumes, grapefruit, and strawberries are some foods that can help Virgos to remain relaxed and calm. Brain foods for Virgos are wild salmon, avocado, and blueberries.

The mineral associated with Virgo is potassium sulfate. It controls the oil in the body. It is necessary for muscle contraction. It also transports oxygen to the cells. It keeps the skin pores open and clean. A lack of this mineral in the body leads to skin and hair problems. Eczema, acne, hair loss, dandruff, and dry skin and hair are symptoms of a deficiency of this mineral. Extreme fatigue and constipation can also occur if one lacks this mineral. Foods that contain this mineral are green leafy vegetables, whole wheat, and whole-grain bread, wheat germ, wheat germ oil, oats, almonds, cheese, oranges, bananas, lemons, lean beef, and lamb. Brussels sprouts, broccoli, cabbage, eggplant, kale, squash, and tomatoes aid in muscle contraction. Melons, apples, pears, and papaya are good hydrating foods for Virgos to eat. Lemon juice will help keep the skin clear and the hair free of dandruff. Cod, salmon, tuna, and shitake mushrooms are the right foods to fight fatigue.

Virgos need to be careful of highly seasoned and spicy foods in their diet so they won't have digestive issues. They should, however, include some spices in their diet because it keeps their food interesting. Basil and lemon balm are known as relaxing seasonings, and they can help the Virgo personality stay calm. Rosemary is also good for the hair, and marjoram and ginger are suitable for the muscles. Mint can prevent anxiety. Virgos should use honey instead of sugar. It prevents constipation. Some herbs and spices that benefit Virgos are chicories, cinnamon, sesame, and turmeric.

Virgos like fresh fruit for desserts, and they do well with light custards and puddings. However, Virgos occasionally crave chocolate. Dark chocolate is a soothing food, and it can relax Virgos.

Like Geminis, Virgos should stay away from caffeinated drinks like coffee and tea because they will get overstimulated. Virgos should drink decaffeinated teas like chamomile, peppermint, and lemon. Virgos do well to drink milk because it can be soothing to their nerves. Alcohol harms Virgos because it is not suitable for the Virgo stomach and liver. Virgos should drink light, dry wine.

Virgos need quiet and relaxation when they eat. It helps calm their nerves which aids in proper digestion.

Virgo Food Guide

Fish

Anchovy
Bass
Bluefish
Carp
Catfish
Cod
Flounder
Grouper
Haddock
Halibut
Herring
Mackerel
Mahi-mahi
Monkfish
Ocean Perch
Orange Roughy
Red Snapper
Sablefish
Salmon
Sardine
Sea Bass
Shark
Smelt
Snapper
Sole
Sturgeon
Swordfish
Trout
Tuna
Turbot
Whitefish
Yellowtail

Seafood

Caviar
Clams
Crab
Crayfish
Lobster
Mussels
Octopus
Oysters
Scallops
Shrimp
Squid

Meat

Lean Red Meats
Veal
Venison

Poultry

Capon
Chicken
Cornish Game Hen
Duck
Goose
Pheasant
Quail
Turkey

Beans (High Carbohydrates)

Black-eyed Peas
Cannellini Beans
Chickpeas
Fava Beans
Garbanzo Beans
Great Northern Beans
Green Peas
Kidney
Lentils
Lima Beans
Navy Beans
Pinto Beans
Red Beans
Split Peas
White Beans

Grains/Breads/Cereals/Pastas

Amaranth
Barley
Bran
Brown Rice
Kamut
Millet
Oats
Pumpernickel
Spelt
Tabbouleh
Wheat

Whole-Grain Foods

Buckwheat
Rye

Cheese/Dairy Products

Butter
Cheeses
Sour Cream

Cream
Eggs
Yogurt
Milk

Oils

Coconut Oil
Fish Oil
Flax Seed Oil
Olive Oil
Peanut Oil
Safflower Oil
Sesame Oil
Vegetable Oil
Wheat Germ Oil

Vegetables

Alfalfa Sprouts
Artichokes
Arugula
Asparagus
Cucumbers
Dandelion Greens
Eggplant
Endive
Peppers
Potatoes
Pumpkin
Radish

Bean sprouts
Beets
Beet Greens
Broccoli
Brussels Sprouts
Cabbage
Cauliflower
Carrots
Celery
Collard Greens
Green Beans
Hops
Kale
Leeks
Lettuces
Mushrooms
Mustard Greens
Okra
Onions
Parsnip
Spinach
Squash
Swiss Chard
Turnip
Turnip Greens
Watercress
Wax Beans
White Beets
Yellow Beans
Zucchini

Fruit

Apples
Apricots
Avocados
Bananas
Blackberries
Blueberries
Boysenberries
Coconut
Cranberries
Dried fruit
Grapefruit
Lemon
Lime
Mandarins
Mango
Melons
Nectarines
Olives
Oranges
Papaya
Peaches
Pears
Plums
Pomegranate
Raisins
Raspberries
Strawberries
Tangerines
Tomatoes

Herbs and Spices

Anise
Basil
Caraway
Cardamom
Caraway
Chicory
Cilantro
Cinnamon
Clove
Coriander
Cumin
Dill
Fennel
Garlic
Ginger
Lemon balm
Licorice
Marjoram
Mint
Nutmeg
Oregano
Parsley
Rosemary
Sage
Sesame
Tarragon
Thyme
Turmeric
Vanilla

Beverages

Decaffeinated Herbal Teas
Light dry wine
Milk
Water

Other

All Types of Nuts
Honey

Virgo Food Recipes

Virgos can be prone to digestion issues because they have sensitive stomachs. They usually like to eat lighter, easy-to-digest foods, including many fruits and vegetables.

Veal Francaise

Serves 6

1½ lbs veal cutlets
¾ tsp salt
½ tsp black pepper
1¾ cup flour
2 large eggs, beaten
½ cup butter, melted
1 cup heavy cream
¾ cup chicken broth
½ cup Chablis wine
¼ cup butter
2 Tbsp fresh lemon juice
1 Tbsp minced fresh parsley
1 lemon, thinly sliced

In one bowl, add the flour. In a second bowl, add the eggs and beat.

Place the veal cutlets between 2 sheets of wax paper. Flatten with a meat mallet to ¼ inch thickness. Sprinkle with salt and pepper. Dredge the cutlets in the flour. Dip the veal in beaten eggs. Dredge one more time in flour.

Melt ½ cup butter in a large skillet over medium heat. Add the veal and sauté for 3 minutes on each side. Remove the veal. Reserve the drippings in the skillet. Set aside and keep warm.

Add the chicken broth, cream, wine, ¼ cp melted butter, and lemon juice to the skillet. Stir well. Bring to a boil over medium heat. Stir frequently. Return the reserved veal to the skillet. Reduce the heat. Simmer uncovered for 5 minutes.

Place the veal on a large serving platter. Place lemon slices on the veal. Sprinkle with parsley and serve.

Grilled Chicken Satay

Serves 4

1 lb boneless skinless chicken breasts

½ cup hoisin sauce

½ cup plum sauce

3 Tbsp green onion, sliced

1 Tbsp grated ginger root

3 Tbsp dry sherry

2 Tbsp white vinegar

Trim fat from chicken breasts. Cut chicken lengthwise into ½ inch strips.

Add all the ingredients except the chicken in a large glass bowl. Add the chicken and toss to coat. Cover and refrigerate for 2 hours.

Set oven to broil.

Drain the chicken from the marinade. Reserve the marinade. Thread 2 pieces of chicken on each of twelve 10-inch skewers. Place on the rack in the broiler pan.

Broil with tops 3 to 4 inches from heat for 4 minutes. Turn and broil for an additional 4 minutes.

Heat the marinade to boiling in 1-quart saucepan. Serve with the chicken.

Lemon Piccata Whitefish

Serves 4

1 lb trout fillets

¾ cup all-purpose flour

1 tsp lemon pepper

Salt

3 Tbsp vegetable oil

2 cloves garlic, minced

1½ cups dry white wine

2 tsp lemon zest

¼ cup lemon juice

2 Tbsp capers, drained

3 Tbsp butter

1 Tbsp fresh parsley, chopped

Preheat oven to 200 degrees Fahrenheit.

Place a serving platter into the oven to warm.

In a shallow bowl, add the flour, lemon pepper, and salt. Firmly press the trout fillets into the seasoned flour. Coat both sides. Shake off excess.

Heat the vegetable oil in a large skillet over medium heat. Pan fry the fish in hot oil for 2 minutes on each side. Turn. Fish should be golden brown. Place the fillet on the warm plate in the oven to keep warm.

Keep a thin film of oil in the skillet and discard the rest. Add the garlic and cook for 20 seconds. Pour the wine into the skillet. Dissolve the brown bits of food into the wine. Add the lemon zest. Bring to a boil. Cook until sauce reduces to about ⅔ cup. Stir often. Add the lemon juice and capers. Cook for 5 more minutes. Sauce should slightly thicken. Add butter. Whisk.

Place trout fillets in the sauce. Turn to coat. Garnish with parsley and serve on the warm plate.

Vegetable Lasagna with White Sauce

Serves 4 to 6

1 head cauliflower, chopped

4 Tbsp butter

½ cup flour

1 cup half and half

2 cups skim milk

¾ cup Parmesan cheese, shredded

¾ cup Swiss cheese, shredded

2 Tbsp Dijon mustard

Pinch of nutmeg

½ tsp salt

1 package no-boil lasagna noodles

2 packages portabella mushrooms, sliced

1 large bunch kale, chopped

1 butternut squash, peeled and thinly sliced

3 cloves garlic, minced

¾ cup Parmesan cheese, shredded

2½ cups Mozzarella, shredded

Preheat oven to 350 degrees Fahrenheit.

Chop cauliflower into small florets and place in small roasting pan. Add a drizzle of olive oil and ⅓ cup water. Season with salt and pepper. Cover with foil and bake for 45 minutes. Cauliflower should be soft. Remove from oven and let cool. Transfer to a food processor and puree until smooth.

Melt butter in a large saucepan over medium heat. Add the flour and stir. Add the half and half and milk. Whisk. Add the Parmesan and Swiss cheeses. Stir. Add the mustard and nutmeg. Fold in the cauliflower puree. Stir well. Season with additional salt.

Preheat oven to 375 degrees Fahrenheit.

Place 3 no-boil lasagna noodles in the base of the pan. Top with ¼ of vegetable mixture. Spoon several scoops of white sauce over the vegetables and sprinkle lightly with Parmesan and Mozzarella. You will need to visually divide the sauce and cheeses into sixths for the remaining layers.

Bake for 35 minutes. Cheese should be a light golden brown.

Bouillabaisse

Serves 6 to 8

1 lb live lobster (1 to 1¼ lbs)

2 large tomatoes, peeled and coarsely chopped

1 large onion, chopped

5 cloves garlic, chopped

¾ cup extra-virgin olive oil

1½ lbs boiling potatoes

½ cup anise, finely chopped

1 bay leaf

1 Tbsp coarse sea salt

¾ tsp black pepper

10 cups whitefish stock (or buy from store)

3 lbs fish fillets (monkfish, turbot, red snapper, striped bass, grouper and/or cod)

½ lb hard-shelled clams, scrubbed

½ lb mussels, scrubbed and debearded

½ lb large shrimp in shells

Croutons

Plunge the lobster headfirst into a 6 to 8-quart pot of boiling water. Cover and cook for 2 minutes.

Transfer the lobster to a colander and let stand until it cools enough to handle. Discard the hot water in the pot.

Place the lobster in a shallow baking pan. Twist off the claws. Crack the claws with a mallet or rolling pin. Separate the claws from the knuckles. Halve body and tail lengthwise through shell with kitchen shears. Cut crosswise through the shell into 2-inch pieces. Reserve the lobster juices in the baking pan.

Add the tomatoes, onion, and garlic in the olive oil in cleaned 6 to 8-quart pot over. Cook over moderate heat for 7 minutes.

Peel the potatoes and cut into ½ inch cubes. Add the potatoes, anise, bay leaf, sea salt, and pepper to the tomatoes. Stir. Add the fish stock. Bring to a boil. Reduce heat. Cover and simmer to 8 to 10 minutes. Potatoes should be tender.

Add thick pieces of fish and clams to the soup. Cover and simmer for 2 minutes. Stir in the mussels, shrimp, lobster, including juices, and remaining fish. Cover and simmer for 5 minutes. Mussels and clams should be wide open. Discard any mussels and clams that do not open.

Pour bouillabaisse in deep soup bowls. Add croutons and serve.

French Onion Soup

Serves 4 to 6

¾ cup unsalted butter
4 onions, sliced
3 garlic cloves, chopped
1 bay leaf
2 fresh thyme leaves
Salt
Freshly ground pepper
2 cups red wine,
3 heaping tablespoons all-purpose flour
2 quarts beef broth
2 to 3 baguettes, sliced
¾ lb grated Gruyere cheese

Melt the butter in a large pot over medium heat. Add the onions, garlic, bay leaf, thyme, salt, and pepper, and cook. Cook for 25 minutes. Onions should be soft and caramelized.

Add the wine to the pot. Bring to a boil. Reduce the heat. Simmer for 5 minutes. Wine should be evaporated and the onions should be dry. Discard the bay leaves and thyme sprigs. Dust the onions with the flour and give them a stir. Turn the heat down to medium-low. Cook for 10 minutes. Add the beef broth. Simmer for 10 minutes. Season with salt and pepper.

Preheat the broiler.

Arrange the baguette slices on a baking sheet in a single layer. Sprinkle the slices with the Gruyere cheese. Broil for 3 to 5 minutes. Cheese should be bubbly and baguettes should be golden brown. Ladle the soup into bowls and float several of the Gruyere croutons on top.

Green Salad Mixed with Grapefruit and Cranberries

Serves 8

2 red grapefruit
½ cup extra-virgin olive oil
2 Tbsp scallions, minced
1 Tbsp white-wine vinegar
½ tsp salt
½ freshly ground pepper
8 cups butter lettuce
8 cups baby spinach
1 14-oz can hearts of palm, drained and cut into bite-size pieces
½ cup dried cranberries
½ cup toasted pine nuts

Remove the skin and white pith from grapefruit with a sharp knife. Working over a bowl, cut the segments from their surrounding membranes. Cut the segments in half on a cutting board. Transfer to a large bowl. Squeeze the grapefruit peel and membranes over the original bowl to extract ¼ cup grapefruit juice. Add the olive oil, scallions, vinegar, salt, and pepper into the bowl with the grapefruit juice.

Add lettuce, spinach, and hearts of palm to the salad bowl with the grapefruit segments.

Toss the salad with the dressing and coat well. Sprinkle with cranberries and pine nuts on top.

Oatmeal Cookies

Makes about 24 cookies

1¼ cups sugar

½ cup sugar

½ cup all-purpose flour

¾ tsp vanilla extract

¼ tsp salt

1¾ cups oats

Beat the sugar and butter in an electric blender. Add the flour, vanilla extract, and salt. Stir in the oats. Blend well.

Cover and refrigerate the cookie dough 1 hour.

Preheat oven to 350 degrees Fahrenheit.

Line 2 baking sheets with parchment paper. Roll dough by tablespoonfuls between palms into balls. Place dough balls on baking sheets, spacing 3 inches apart. Flatten cookies.

Bake for 10 or 11 minutes. Cookies should be golden brown.

Let the cookies remain on the cookie sheets for 1 minute. Transfer the cookies to cooling racks and cool completely.

Libra (September 23 to October 22)

Like Taurus, Libra is ruled by the planet Venus. Venus is the planet of love and beauty. Venus governs art.

The symbol associated with Libra is the scales. The scales represent balance and justice.

The colors associated with Libra are blue and lavender. These colors represent harmony, refinement, and romance.

Libra is a cardinal air sign. Cardinal signs are natural leaders. They are open to change and can make an impact. Because Air signs lead with their head, they are intellectually inclined and are good with ideas. Libras are bright-minded. They like new projects and different ideas. They like to find solutions to problems.

Libra is a positive masculine sign.

Libra rules the kidneys, lumbar region (which includes the lower spine and back), and buttocks. Venus, the planet that rules Libra, rules the skin, hair, veins, and throat.

Libra is depicted as the Goddess of Justice. Libras have strong opinions regarding what is right and what is wrong. They are born diplomats. Libras are idealistic, and they strive to work for peace. Libras do well when working in a group because they are team players. They strive for cooperation and compromise because they don't like disharmony. They are good listeners and can work through problems because of their objectivity and impartiality in making decisions.

Because of the Venus influence, Libras are elegant, polished, charming, and artistic. They have exquisite taste, and their homes are usually beautifully adorned. Libras are easygoing and friendly, and they like to entertain in style.

Because of their superior intellect, Libras typically have a broad range of interests and can talk about many things. Gifted with imagination and flair, Libras have an open and independent mind. People are attracted to Libras because they are affectionate, romantic, warmhearted, and like to please others.

Libras usually have good health because of their concern to stay attractive. Being ruled by Venus, Libras are good-looking people. They have oval-shaped faces and long, elegant necks. They have almond-shaped eyes and a V-shaped chin. Libras have dark hair with a good texture. They have good skin even though it can be sensitive. They also have good bone structure and well-built physiques. They are average to tall and are of average build. Graceful lower spines and curvaceous buttocks help identify Libra women, and well-shaped muscular backs help identify Libra men. Libras like to dress well and wear expensive perfumes. Libras like to exercise if they have a partner. Tennis, golf, and bicycle riding are good sports for Libras.

Libra represents partnerships, relationships, and marriage. The dominant keywords for Libras are "I BALANCE." Their dominant trait is their charm. Some famous people born under the sign of Libra are Truman Capote, Ray Charles, Michael Douglas, Dwight D. Eisenhower, Mohandas K. Gandhi, Jesse Jackson, John Lennon, Walter Matthau, Gwyneth Paltrow, Mario Puzo, Christopher Reeve, Will Smith, Bruce Springsteen, Sting, Margaret Thatcher, and Barbara Walters.

Libras have a moderate appetite, but since they like parties and are social, they often eat more than they should. They are connoisseurs of good food and drink because they approach food passionately. They are open to trying exotic and new cuisines. Libras prefer light, elegant foods delicately seasoned. They don't like foods with intense flavors. Libras are known to like delicate dishes and haute cuisine. Beautifully presented food makes a significant impact on a Libra.

Like everything else in a Libra's life, balance is the key to their health and well-being. Food is the central area Libras need to watch since one of their weak points is the kidneys. For this reason, Libras do very well when following a vegetarian diet. Libras also do well with a low-fat and sugar-free diet. Broiled fish, seafood, poultry, low-fat cheeses, yogurt, and whole-grain bread are also suitable for Libras. Libras should not overeat beef or pork.

Libras should eat cabbage and celery. These foods help keep the kidneys flushed out. Grapes are good for Libras because they reduce pressure on the kidneys by eliminating acid from the body. Bananas, blueberries, and cranberries are also good foods for Libras. They prevent kidney stones.

Artichokes, avocados, cherries, green beans, mangos, pears, peaches, dried fruit, peas, and almonds help oxidize the skin. Libras should eat these foods to maintain good skin. Pumpkin seeds and walnuts are suitable for the hair.

The mineral associated with Libra is sodium phosphate. It balances the acids and alkaline in the body and does away with its waste material. Too much acid in the body can impair kidney function, so Libras must keep their bodies properly balanced. One can tell if there is a deficiency of sodium phosphate in their diet because their skin can get yellowish or sallow. Apples, asparagus, beets, carrots, corn, radishes, spinach, raisins, strawberries, tomatoes, brown rice, oatmeal, and wheat are good food sources for sodium phosphate. Other foods that promote balance are blackberries, raspberries, mangos, pumpkins, squash, sweet potatoes, and yams.

Herbs and spices that are good for Libras to use are basil, cardamom, cinnamon, fennel, and parsley because they promote proper kidney function. Mint, thyme, and vanilla benefit Libras because they are suitable for balance. Other herbs and spices good for Libras are anises, caraway, clove, dill, garlic, ginger, marjoram, nutmeg, rosemary, sage, and tarragon.

Even though Libras are conscious about their weight, they have a weakness for sweets. Libras love all things decadent, so it is no wonder they love desserts. Libras love ice creams with lots of toppings. They also like light fruity desserts.

Libras should drink plenty of drink water and fruit juices to keep their kidneys flushed out. They should stay away from caffeine because it will make them feel out of sorts and unbalanced. Libras like to drink wine. Sometimes a sweet white wine can keep Libras nicely balanced.

When dining, the people and the environment mean more to Libras than the food.

Libra Food Guide

Fish

Anchovy
Bass
Bluefish
Carp
Catfish
Cod
Flounder
Grouper
Haddock
Halibut
Herring
Mackerel
Mahi-mahi
Monkfish
Ocean Perch
Orange Roughy
Red Snapper
Sablefish
Salmon
Sardine
Sea Bass
Shark
Smelt
Snapper
Sole
Sturgeon
Swordfish
Trout
Tuna
Turbot
Whitefish
Yellowtail

Seafood

Caviar
Clams
Crab
Crayfish
Lobster
Mussels
Octopus
Oysters
Scallops
Shrimp
Squid

Meat

Lean Red Meats
Veal
Venison

Poultry

Capon
Chicken
Cornish Game Hen
Duck
Goose
Pheasant
Quail
Turkey

Beans (High Carbohydrates)

Black-eyed Peas
Cannellini Beans
Chickpeas
Fava Beans
Garbanzo Beans
Great Northern Beans
Green Peas
Kidney
Lentils
Lima Beans
Navy Beans
Pinto Beans
Red Beans
Split Peas
White Beans

Grains/Breads/Cereals/Pastas

Amaranth
Barley
Bran
Brown Rice
Kamut
Millet
Oats
Pumpernickel
Spelt
Tabbouleh
Wheat

Whole-Grains

Buckwheat
Rye

Cheese/Dairy Products

Butter
Cheeses (low fat)
Cream (low fat
Eggs
Milk (low fat)
Sour Cream (low fat)
Yogurt (low fat)

Oils

Coconut Oil
Fish Oil
Flax Seed Oil
Olive Oil
Peanut Oil
Safflower Oil
Sesame Oil
Vegetable Oil
Wheat Germ Oil

Vegetables

Alfalfa Sprouts
Artichokes
Arugula
Asparagus
Bean Sprouts
Beets
Beet Greens
Broccoli
Brussels Sprouts
Cabbage
Cauliflower
Carrots
Celery
Collard Greens
Peppers
Cucumbers
Dandelion Greens
Eggplant
Endive
Green Beans
Hops
Kale
Leeks
Lettuces
Mushrooms
Mustard Greens
Okra
Onions
Parsnip
Potatoes
Pumpkin
Radish
Spinach
Squash
Swiss Chard
Turnip
Turnip Greens
Watercress
Wax Beans
White Beets
Yellow Beans
Zucchini
Corn

Fruit

Apples
Apricots
Avocados
Bananas
Blackberries
Blueberries
Boysenberries
Cherries
Coconut
Cranberries
Dried fruit
Grapes
Grapefruit
Lemon
Lime
Mandarins
Mango
Melons
Nectarines
Olives
Oranges
Papaya
Peaches
Pears
Plums
Pomegranate
Raisins
Raspberries
Strawberries
Tangerines
Tomatoes

Herbs and Spices

Anise
Basil
Caraway
Cayenne
Cardamom
Cilantro
Cinnamon
Clove
Dill
Fennel
Garlic
Ginger
Lemongrass
Marjoram
Mint
Nutmeg
Oregano
Parsley
Parsley
Rosemary
Sage
Sesame
Tarragon
Thyme
Vanilla

Beverages

Decaffeinated Coffee
Decaffeinated Herbal Teas
Fruit Juices
Red Wine
Water
White Wine

Other

Almonds
Chestnuts
Pecans
Pumpkin seeds
Sesame seeds
Walnuts

Libra Recipes

Libras enjoy eating a little bit of everything for their meals, even though they prefer sweets and chocolates, and would skip the main course for dessert, if necessary.

Beef Stew

Serves 4

3½ lbs beef chuck roast, trimmed, cut into 1-inch pieces
3 medium onions, chopped
6 cloves garlic, thinly sliced
6 thyme sprigs

3 tsp thyme leaves, finely chopped

3 bay leaves

1 cup olive oil

1 bottle dry red wine

Salt

Freshly ground black pepper

¾ cup dried porcini mushrooms

1 cup red port wine

2 Tbsp tomato paste

½ cup extra-virgin olive oil

4 slices bacon, thick-cut, cut into 1-inch pieces

3 celery ribs, finely chopped

¾ cup all-purpose flour

3 large carrots, cut into 1-inch pieces

6 large shitake mushrooms, stems discarded, caps thinly sliced

3 cups chicken stock

2 Tbsp flat-leaf parsley, minced

In a large bowl, toss the beef chuck with the onions, garlic, thyme sprigs, bay leaves, olive oil, and 1 cup of the red wine. Add salt and pepper to season. Cover with plastic wrap and refrigerate overnight.

Drain the meat. Place the meat on a plate lined with a paper towel. Pat the meat dry. Reserve the onion mixture.

In a medium heatproof bowl, cover the dried porcini with the wine. Microwave at high power for 1 minute. Porcini should be softened. Let cool. Using a slotted spoon, transfer the porcini to a food processor. Add the tomato paste and half of the porcini soaking liquid to the food processor. Process until smooth. Reserve the remaining porcini soaking liquid.

In a large, heavy casserole, heat 2 tablespoons of the extra-virgin olive oil. Add the bacon and cook over moderately high heat for 5 minutes. Bacon should be crisp. Add the reserved onion mixture and celery and cook over moderately high heat for 8 minutes. Stir occasionally. Onion-bacon mixture should be softened. Using a slotted spoon, transfer the onion-bacon mixture to a bowl.

Heat the remaining 2 tablespoons of olive oil in the casserole. Dust the meat with flour. Shake off the excess. Add half of the meat to the casserole. Cook over moderately high heat for 10 minutes. Meat should be browned. Transfer the meat to the bowl with the onion-bacon mixture. Lower the heat to moderate. Brown the remaining meat.

Return all the meat and the onion mixture to the casserole. Stir until sizzling. Add the porcini paste. Stir for 1 minute. Stir in the carrots and sliced shiitake cap mushrooms. Add the stock, the remaining red wine, and the remaining porcini soaking liquid. Bring to a boil. Add salt and pepper to season. Cover and simmer over low heat for about 2 hours. Meat should be tender. Discard the thyme sprigs and bay leaves.

Uncover the stew and cook over moderate heat for 10 minutes. Sauce should be slightly thickened. Add the parsley and 2 teaspoons of chopped thyme. Add salt and pepper to season.

Lemon Sage Chicken

Serves 6

2 lbs chicken pieces

¼ cup extra virgin olive oil

½ cup lemon juice

1 Tbsp lemon zest

4 Tbsp chopped fresh sage

2 cloves garlic, crushed and chopped

1 tsp salt

1 tsp ground black pepper

In a large bowl, combine the olive oil, lemon juice, lemon zest, sage, garlic, salt, and pepper. Pour this marinade into a large glass baking dish. Add the chicken to the dish. Turn the chicken pieces once to coat with the marinade. Cover the dish and refrigerate the chicken for 1 hour. Turn the chicken pieces once every 15 minutes.

Preheat a grill or brush a large skillet with oil and set it over medium-high heat. Arrange all the chicken pieces on the grill or place the chicken, in batches, into the hot skillet. Discard the marinade.

Cook the chicken for 4 to 6 minutes on each side. The chicken is done when the thickest part feels firm to the touch.

Wasabi Trout

Serves 4

4 4-oz trout fillets

½ cup soy sauce

2 Tbsp olive oil

2½ tsp wasabi paste

2 tsp minced garlic

¼ tsp crushed oregano

1 pinch ground black pepper

1 pinch Cajun seasoning

Preheat oven to 450 degrees Fahrenheit.

Line a baking dish with aluminum foil. Grease with olive oil.

In a medium bowl, mix together the soy sauce, olive oil, wasabi paste, garlic, oregano, and black pepper.

Cut a diagonal slash across each piece of fish. Coat the fish with the wasabi mixture. Add the remaining wasabi mixture over the fish and into the diagonal cuts.

Place the fish into the prepared baking dish. Sprinkle with Cajun seasoning.

Bake for 7 to 10 minutes. Fish should be opaque and flake easily.

Escargot with Garlic Butter

Serves 6

6 Tbsp softened butter

2 tsp shallots, finely chopped

3 cloves garlic, crushed and finely chopped

2 Tbsp celery, finely chopped

1 Tbsp parsley, finely chopped fresh

¼ tsp salt

¼ tsp ground black pepper

12 large mushrooms, cleaned with stems removed

12 large canned snails

Preheat an oven to 375 degrees Fahrenheit.

In a large bowl, mix the butter, shallots, garlic, celery, parsley, salt, and pepper.

Place a small spoonful of the herb butter and a snail in each mushroom cap. Brush the exterior of the mushroom with a bit of the herb butter.

Arrange the mushrooms in a shallow baking dish. Bake for 15 minutes. Serve hot.

Steamed Mussels in Vermouth

Serves 4

3 Tbsp butter or margarine

1 Tbsp olive oil

2 Tbsp onions, finely chopped

2 Tbsp celery, finely chopped

2 Tbsp carrots, finely chopped

2 medium shallots, sliced thinly

2 cloves garlic, crushed and chopped

1½ tsp fresh tarragon, chopped

1 tsp parsley, finely chopped

½ tsp salt

¼ tsp ground black pepper

½ cup vermouth

1 cup dry white wine

In a large skillet, over medium heat, melt the butter. Add the olive oil, onions, carrots, celery, shallots, and garlic. Sauté for 5 minutes. The mixture should be tender. Add the tarragon, parsley, salt, and pepper to the skillet. Cook for 1 minute.

Add the vermouth and white wine to the skillet. Bring to a simmer. Add the mussels to the wine sauce. Turn the heat up a little. Cover and steam the mussels for 5 to 10 minutes. Mussels should be opened. Discard any mussels that do not open.

Serve the mussels hot with the wine sauce.

Tuna Tataki

Serves 4

¼ cup ginger, minced
¼ cup sesame seeds
1 Tbsp cracked black pepper
½ lb very fresh, sushi-grade ahi tuna
Kosher salt
3 Tbsp peanut oil, for searing
1 Tbsp lime juice
1 medium-size, ripe avocado, peeled, pitted, quartered and sliced
2½ cups mixed greens
10 thin slices red onion
1 medium tomato, peeled, seeded, and diced
1 small shallot, minced
½ tsp finely grated fresh ginger
Freshly ground black pepper
½ cup soy sauce
½ cup lime juice
½ cup olive oil

To make the ginger sauce, combine the shallot, ginger, a few grinds pepper, soy sauce, and lime juice in a small bowl. Add the olive oil and whisk. Set aside. Whisk again when ready to serve.

On a shallow plate, mix together the ginger, sesame seeds, and cracked black pepper.

Season the tuna with salt. Make ½ inch deep slices in the tuna, every ¼ to ½ inch or so to make it easier to slice at the end. Roll the tuna in the ginger mixture, pressing lightly so the mixture sticks to the tuna.
Place a sauté pan over high heat. Add the oil. Sear the tuna on both sides for 30 seconds. Remove the tuna from the pan and set aside. Deglaze the pan with lime juice. Pour the lime juice over the tuna.
In a medium bowl, combine the avocado, greens, red onion, and tomato. Toss with some of the ginger sauce.

Slice the tuna.

Place some of the dressed greens on 4 plates. Top with sliced tuna. Drizzle with more of the ginger sauce.

Spinach Artichoke Lasagna

Serves 6 to 8

1 can quartered artichoke hearts, drained

1 10-oz package frozen chopped spinach

½ stick butter

1½ cups flour

3 cups milk

Pinch nutmeg

Pinch salt

Pinch white pepper

4 cups Mozzarella cheese

½ cup Parmesan cheese

1 package no-boil lasagna noodles

Walnuts, optional

Preheat oven to 350 degrees Fahrenheit.

Spray a 9 x13 inch baking dish with cooking spray.

Chop artichokes in blender or food processor. Squeeze out liquid from the spinach.

Melt the butter in large frying pan. Add the flour. Cook for 1 to 2 minutes. Add the milk slowly. Stir constantly until a thickness occurs. Add the nutmeg, salt, and white pepper. Stir. Add artichokes and spinach. Heat through.

Spread some of the artichoke mixture in the bottom of the prepared baking dish. Top with a layer of lasagna noodles. Then top noodles with a layer of Mozzarella cheese. Repeat layers 2 more times. End with the artichoke mixture and Mozzarella cheese. Sprinkle Parmesan cheese on top.

Bake for 30 to 45 minutes. Lasagna should be heated through and bubbly.

Top with walnuts and more Parmesan cheese if desired.

Avocado and Romaine Salad

Serves 2 to 4

1½ cups cherry tomatoes, halved

1 Tbsp fresh chives, chopped

1½ cups avocado, chopped

3½ cups chopped romaine hearts

3 tsp fresh parsley, chopped

1 tsp fresh dill weed, chopped

Balsamic vinegar

Extra-virgin olive oil

In a large bowl, add all the ingredients. Toss. Add two tablespoons of olive oil to one tablespoon of vinegar. Toss again.

Add more olive oil and vinegar as needed.

Orange Vinaigrette Glazed Beets

Serves 6

1 lb whole beets, scrubbed with ½ inch of stem left

1½ tsp cornstarch

½ cup orange juice

1 Tbsp balsamic vinegar

1 Tbsp orange marmalade

¼ tsp ground black pepper

In a large skillet or pot, steam the beets for 35 minutes.

Trim the ends and remove the skin. Quarter the peeled beets. Set aside.

In a small saucepan, dissolve the cornstarch in the orange juice. Turn the heat on low-medium. Stir the balsamic vinegar, orange marmalade, and black pepper into the saucepan. Bring the glaze to a simmer for 1 minute.

Remove from heat and toss the beets into the glaze.

Green Beans with Almonds

Serves 8

2 lbs green beans, trimmed

½ stick butter or margarine

½ tsp salt

½ cup slivered almonds, lightly toasted

Add the green beans to a large pot of boiling salted water. Cook for 5 minutes. Beans should be crisp-tender. Drain the beans and transfer them to a large bowl of ice water. Cool completely. Drain the beans.

Add the beans into a skillet and steam for 5 minutes.

Melt the butter in a large, heavy skillet over medium-high heat. Add the beans to the skillet and toss for about 5 minutes. Beans should be heated through.

Transfer to a serving bowl. Sprinkle with toasted almonds.

Diced Grilled Watermelon

Serves 4

4 oz rice wine vinegar
½ Tbsp chopped ginger
½ stalk lemongrass, smashed and chopped
2 Tbsp sugar
20 oz seedless watermelon, skin on, sliced ¾ inch thick

In a saucepan, add the rice wine vinegar, ginger, lemongrass, and sugar. Bring to a boil. Turn off and let it cool down. Marinate the watermelon in syrup for 2 hours.

Rotate the watermelon every half hour so that all sides are equally marinated.

In a hot grill, sear each slice of watermelon for 2 minutes on both sides.

Remove from grill. Remove the skin. Cut in large slices.

Chestnut Soup

Serves 10

4 cups vegetable stock

8 oz cooked chestnuts

2 cups white onions, chopped

1 cup carrots, chopped

1 cup celery, chopped

½ tsp salt

¼ tsp ground black pepper

1 cup plus ¼ cup crème fraise, divided

In a large saucepan, simmer the vegetable stock, chestnuts, onions, carrots, celery, salt, and pepper over medium-high heat. Cover the pan. Reduce the heat to low-medium. Simmer the soup for 30 minutes. Vegetables should be tender. Stir in 1 cup of the crème fraise.

Add the soup in batches to a blender. Process the soup batches until smooth.

Spoon the soup into serving bowls while hot.

Garnish with the remaining crème fraise and serve.

White Bean Soup

Serves 4

4 Tbsp extra-virgin olive oil

2 medium onions, diced

4 stalks celery, diced

2 15.5-oz cans cannellini beans, drained and rinsed

4 cups low-sodium chicken broth

6 cloves garlic, minced

½ cup fresh cilantro, chopped

1 bunch Swiss chard, chopped

1½ tsp salt (preferably Kosher)

Salt

Freshly ground pepper

In a medium pot, heat 1 tablespoon olive oil over medium-high heat. Add the onions, celery and 1½ teaspoon salt and cook for 5 minutes. Vegetables should be golden brown. Add the beans and chicken broth. Bring to a simmer and cook for 15 minutes.

Meanwhile, in a large skillet, heat the remaining 3 tablespoons olive oil over medium heat. Add the garlic and cilantro and cook for 2 minutes. Garlic should be soft. Add the Swiss chard and stir. Cover and cook for 2 minutes. Swiss chard should be wilted.

Scrape the contents of the skillet into the pot. Simmer for 5 minutes or until heated through. Add salt and pepper to season.

Apple Cake

Makes 1 cake

2¼ cups sugar
4 eggs
1 tsp vanilla extract
7 cups Golden Delicious apples, chopped
2½ tsp baking powder
2 Tbsp baking soda
½ tsp salt
¾ cup raisins, optional

Preheat oven to 325 degrees Fahrenheit.

Grease a 9 x 13 x 3 cooking pan.

In a large bowl, mix the wet ingredients. Add the apples, flour, raisins, and the other dry ingredients. Mix well.

Add the mixture to the prepared cooking pan.

Bake for 1 hour.

Pumpkin Ice Cream Dessert

Serves 6

1 15-oz can pumpkin

1 cup white sugar

1 tsp salt

½ tsp ground ginger

½ tsp ground cinnamon

½ tsp ground nutmeg

1½ cups pecans, chopped

½ gallon vanilla ice cream, softened

38 vanilla wafers or gingersnaps

Line 9 x 13-inch dish or a sealable plastic container with 18 vanilla wafers or gingersnaps.

In a large bowl, add the pumpkin, sugar, salt, ginger, cinnamon, and nutmeg. Mix well. Add the pecans. Stir. Add the ice cream.

Spread half of the ice cream mixture over the cookies. Repeat layering.

Freeze until firm.

Berry Pudding Trifle

Serves 14

1½ cups cold fat-free milk

1 package sugar-free instant vanilla pudding mix

1 cup fat-free vanilla yogurt

8 oz reduced-fat cream cheese, cubed

1 cup reduced-fat sour cream

1 tsp vanilla extract

12 oz frozen reduced-fat whipped topping, thawed, divided

1 18-inch prepared angel food cake, cut into 1-inch cubes

1 pint each blackberries, raspberries, and blueberries

In a small bowl, add the milk and pudding mix. Whisk for 2 minutes. Let stand for 2 minutes. Mixture should be soft-set.

In a large bowl, add the yogurt, cream cheese, sour cream, and vanilla. Beat until smooth. Fold in the pudding mixture and 1 cup whipped topping.

Place a third of the cake cubes in a 4-quart trifle bowl. Add ⅓ of the pudding mixture. Then add ⅓ of the berries. Then add ½ of the remaining whipped topping. Repeat layers once. Top with the remaining cake, pudding, and berries.

Serve immediately or refrigerate.

Scorpio (October 23 to November 21)

Scorpio is ruled by the planet Pluto. Pluto is intense and powerful. It deals with regeneration.

The symbol associated with Scorpio is the Scorpion. The Scorpion is a secretive sea creature that can sting, poison, and kill its enemies.

The colors associated with Scorpio are crimson, burgundy, and maroon. These colors represent passion.

Scorpio is a fixed water sign. Fixed signs are steady and stable. Fixed signs show determination. Water signs are sensitive, and their emotions run deep. Scorpios are persistent and strong-willed. They have an incredible amount of emotional and intellectual depth.

Scorpio is a negative feminine sign.

Scorpio rules the genitals.

Scorpios are intense and magnetic. Filled with desire, Scorpios are motivated and resourceful. They are powerhouses because they can accomplish anything they want due to their solid mental capability. Scorpios never give up, and they never do anything by half-measures. They can be unyielding, subtle, and wise. They don't miss much because of their heightened awareness and intuition. Scorpios ask a lot of questions. They like to probe and get to the bottom of things. They make good investigators. Scorpios are considered one of the most intelligent signs of the zodiac.

Scorpios are the most misunderstood sign of the zodiac. It could be because, like the Scorpion, they are secretive and like controlling their destiny. Scorpios are also complex and highly independent, so getting much out of them isn't easy. Scorpio is also a sign of many contradictions. They can be possessive and jealous in relationships and, at the same time, be very loyal. While presenting a calm face to the world, Scorpios are very emotional deep down. Scorpios have an excellent memory and can hold a grudge forever. They are very generous to those who are kind to them. Scorpios are not shy but can withdraw when their feelings are hurt.

Scorpios use all their energy, drive, and endurance to give their life a deep and meaningful purpose. They are idealists and are an active force in helping others. Scorpios make good doctors, surgeons, scientists, and spiritual leaders. They are passionate in everything they do in life. As challenging and moody as Scorpios can be, they are kind, loving, generous, and loyal people.

Overall, Scorpios are very healthy and strong. Since Pluto is the planet of regeneration, Scorpios are incredibly resistant and blessed with good recuperative and transformation powers. When faced with a health problem, they are quick to recover. Since Pluto represents the body's reproductive system, Scorpios have sturdy, well-built, voluptuous bodies. They often have broad shoulders, square faces, beautiful eyes, and well-defined lips. Their hair is usually brown, thick, and coarse. Scorpios are serious-looking people. Scorpios need strenuous exercise to release their pent-up emotions. Even though Scorpios can be competitive, they like to exercise alone. They enjoy running and swimming. They do well on treadmills and Stairmasters. Scorpios like weight training and gymnastics.

Scorpio represents sex appeal. The dominant keywords for Scorpios are "I DESIRE." Their dominant trait is idealism. Some famous people born under the sign of Scorpio are Johnny Carson, Charles, Prince of Wales, Hillary Rodham Clinton, Walter Cronkite, Danny DeVito, Leonardo DiCaprio, Bill Gates, Whoopi Goldberg, Goldie Hawn, Mahalia Jackson, Robert Kennedy, Julia Roberts, Carl Sagan, Jonas Salk, and Ted Turner.

Scorpios have a hearty appetite. They need to replenish their energy because of their resistant powers and rugged exterior. Because of their intense desires, Scorpios have a love affair with food. A Scorpio's taste buds are complex and very adept at tasting richness. They often eat things that others will not.

On the other hand, Scorpios can go overboard to lose weight. They need to be careful on diets because their obsessive nature and sheer determination can lead them to fad diets and maybe even eating disorders. But because Scorpios have such self-discipline and control, weight loss is easier for them than any other zodiac sign.

A healthy diet is vital to Scorpios to keep up their energy. They should eat foods high in protein, such as meats, poultry, and fish. Scorpios need to eat breakfast and eat smaller meals throughout the day. Their sugar levels will be more balanced, and their food cravings will diminish. Fresh fruits and vegetables help Scorpios maintain balance.

Most likely, Scorpios will eat many pungent flavored, spicy foods. Scorpios are attracted to red curries and spicy tomato sauce. Tandoori chicken is a favorite food of a Scorpio. Being a water sign, Scorpios like fish and all types of seafood. They also like soft and moist food. They like foods that come with a sauce or some other liquid dressing. Foods with smooth textures such as soufflés and pates are all-time favorites of a Scorpio.

Scorpios like to cleanse and detoxify their bodies because of the feeling of regeneration. Foods that help detoxify the body are green, leafy vegetables like broccoli, kale, and mustard greens. Watermelon, strawberries, oranges, pineapples, and mangos also help detoxify the body.

Like Cancer, water is necessary for a Scorpio's life. Too little water causes dehydration, and the skin becomes dry. Asparagus, cauliflower, cucumbers, radishes, and tomatoes are some foods that have a lot of water in them. As mentioned under Cancer, too much water in a person's system slows down digestion and causes weight gain. Whole-grain cereals, dairies, and fresh fruit juices are safe water regulating foods.

The mineral associated with Scorpio is calcium sulfate. It plays a key role in repairing tissues and helps with resistance to infectious diseases. It enables the nose, mouth, throat, esophagus, reproductive organs, and intestinal pathways to function properly. Colds, sinus infections, skin eruptions, and infertility occur when this mineral is deficient in the body. Onions, parsnips, watercress, figs, prunes, black cherries, and coconuts contain high levels of calcium sulfate. Scorpios also need calcium to prevent colds and infections and help heal body tissue. Calcium also helps counteract a Scorpio's moodiness. Foods high in calcium are fish and dairy products and celery, red beets, bananas, and citric fruits.

Basil, cinnamon, curry, garlic, ginger, nutmeg, and paprika have robust flavors that a Scorpio's palate loves. Cardamom, coriander, cumin, horseradish, licorice, mint, mustard, sweet pepper, and vanilla are other herbs and spices most associated with Scorpios. Some other herbs and spices that Scorpios like are caraway, clove, dill, marjoram, oregano, saffron, sage, sesame, tarragon, and turmeric.

Scorpios are confusing when it comes to desserts. Some Scorpios like desserts, and some don't. A dark, rich chocolate mousse is a favorite for those who like desserts. Scorpios also like sweet cream desserts because they are soft and hold moisture.

Water and fresh fruit juices are probably the healthiest drinks for Scorpios because they help keep their body fluids correct. Scorpios love different types of coffees and exotic teas. Scorpios also like wine and brandy. Scorpios need to be careful when drinking. Because of their intensity and moodiness, they can forget about food when they have a problem and turn to alcohol. An occasional glass of wine in the evening won't hurt them.

Scorpios like to sit down to large meals with bitter or extreme flavors.

Scorpio Food Guide

Fish

Anchovy	Mackerel	Smelt
Bass	Mahi-mahi	Snapper
Bluefish	Monkfish	Sole
Carp	Ocean Perch	Sturgeon
Catfish	Orange Roughy	Swordfish
Cod	Red Snapper	Trout
Flounder	Sablefish	Tuna
Grouper	Salmon	Turbot
Haddock	Sardine	Whitefish
Halibut	Sea Bass	Yellowtail
Herring	Shark	

Seafood

Caviar	Lobster	Scallops
Clams	Mussels	Shrimp
Crab	Octopus	Squid
Crayfish	Oysters	

Meat

Bacon	Pork	Veal
Beef	Sausage	Venison
Lamb	Steak	

Poultry

Capon	Duck	Quail
Chicken	Goose	Turkey
Cornish Game Hen	Pheasant	

Beans (High Carbohydrates)

Black-eyed Peas	Great Northern Beans	Navy Beans
Cannellini Beans	Green Peas	Pinto Beans
Chickpeas	Kidney	Red Beans
Fava Beans	Lentils	Split Peas
Garbanzo Beans	Lima Beans	White Beans

Grains/Breads/Cereals/Pastas

Amaranth
Barley
Bran
Brown Rice
Kamut
Millet
Oats
Pumpernickel
Spelt
Tabbouleh
Wheat

Whole-grain foods

Buckwheat
Rye

Cheese/Dairy Products

Butter
Cheeses
Cream
Eggs
Milk
Sour Cream
Yogurt

Oils

Coconut Oil
Fish Oil
Flax Seed Oil
Olive Oil
Peanut Oil
Safflower Oil
Sesame Oil
Vegetable Oil
Wheat Germ Oil

Vegetables

Alfalfa Sprouts
Artichokes
Cucumbers
Dandelion Greens
Potatoes
Pumpkin

Arugula
Asparagus
Bean Sprouts
Beets
Beet greens
Broccoli
Brussels Sprouts
Cabbage
Cauliflower
Carrots
Celery
Collard Greens
Corn
Eggplant
Endive
Green Beans
Hops
Kale
Leeks
Lettuces
Mushrooms
Mustard Greens
Okra
Onions
Parsnip
Peppers
Radish
Spinach
Squash
Swiss Chard
Turnip
Turnip Greens
Watercress
Wax Beans
White Beets
Yellow Beans
Zucchini

Fruit

Apples
Apricots
Avocados
Bananas
Blackberries
Blueberries
Boysenberries
Cherries
Coconut
Cranberries
Dried fruit
Figs
Grapes
Grapefruit
Lemon
Lime
Mandarins
Mango
Melons
Nectarines
Olives
Oranges
Papaya
Peaches
Pears
Plums
Pineapple
Pomegranate
Prunes
Raisins
Raspberries
Strawberries
Tangerines
Tomatoes

Herbs and Spices

Basil
Caraway
Cardamom
Chile peppers
Cilantro
Cinnamon
Clove
Coriander
Cumin
Curry
Dill
Fennel
Garlic
Ginger
Horseradish
Licorice
Marjoram
Mint
Mustard
Nutmeg
Oregano
Paprika
Parsley
Rosemary
Saffron
Sage
Sesame
Sweet Pepper
Tarragon
Thyme
Turmeric
Vanilla

Beverages

Coffee
Brandy
Fruit Juices
Red Wine
Water
White Wine
Tea

Other

Honey
Sesame Seeds

Scorpio Recipes

Scorpios like food that reminds them of themselves—spicy, bold, and unique. Especially during the cold season, Scorpios need to make sure they're getting nutrition along with flavor to ward off illness and skin problems

Caribbean Lamb Chops

Serves 4

8 lamb chops
4 Tbsp cooking oil
Grated rind and juice of 2 limes
1 Tbsp brown sugar
1 tsp ground ginger
Salt
Pepper

In a large bowl, add all the ingredients except the lamb chops. Mix well.

Marinate the lamb chops in the mixture for 2 to 3 hours. Turn occasionally.

Cook the lamb chops under a hot grill for 15 minutes. Turn and baste the chops often with the marinade.

Steak and Ale

Serves 4

4 sirloin steaks, sliced ½ inch
Butter or margarine
1 medium yellow onion, diced
5 oz button mushrooms, sliced
1-pint lager beer
1 tsp dried thyme
1 tsp dried parsley
½ tsp nutmeg
2 sticks butter or margarine
3 Tbsp all-purpose flour
Salt
Pepper

Season the steaks on both sides with salt, pepper, and butter. Put onto a hot grill and brown on both sides.

In a Dutch oven or cast-iron frying pan, add 1 stick of butter, onion, mushrooms, and salt. Cover with lid and allow the mixture to sweat. Add the beer and place steaks in pan. Allow to stew until tender.

In a large bowl, combine the thyme, parsley, nutmeg, the remaining butter, and flour. Add to the steaks and cook until thickened.

Lemon Curry Walnut Chicken

Serves 4

4 skinless, boneless chicken breast halves

¼ cup reduced-sodium soy sauce

¼ cup sherry or red wine

2 tsp vegetable oil

2 Tbsp sugar

1 clove garlic, minced

1 Tbsp grated fresh ginger root or 1 ½ tsp powdered ginger

½ cup fat-free mayonnaise

½ cup plain nonfat yogurt

2 Tbsp lemon juice

2 tsp curry powder

1 clove garlic, minced

Salt

Pepper

1 cup walnuts, chopped

In a medium bowl, add the soy sauce, sherry, oil, sugar, garlic, and ginger root or ginger. Whisk until the sugar has dissolved.

Put the chicken in a large lock-top plastic bag and pour in the marinade. Press the air out and seal the bag tightly. Massage the bag gently to distribute the marinade. Place in a large bowl and refrigerate for at least 2 hours or up to 24 hours. Remove the chicken from the marinade. Reserve the marinade.

Grill chicken over hot coals for 15 minutes. Brush the chicken with the reserved marinade on both sides for the first 10 minutes. If using a broiler, grill the chicken for about 12 to 15 minutes. Brush the chicken on both sides with the reserved marinade for the first 8 minutes.

For the lemon curry sauce, add the mayonnaise, yogurt, lemon juice, curry, and garlic in a small bowl. Stir. Add salt and pepper for seasoning. Add the walnuts. Stir.

Serve the chicken breast halves accompanied by the lemon curry sauce.

Tandoori Chicken

Serves 4 to 6

4 whole chicken legs, skinless, bone-in

3 Tbsp vegetable oil

1 tsp coriander, ground

1 tsp cumin, ground

1 tsp turmeric, ground

1 tsp cayenne

1 Tbsp garam masala

1 Tbsp sweet paprika

1½ cups plain yogurt

2 Tbsp lemon juice

5 garlic cloves, minced

2 Tbsp fresh ginger, minced

1 tsp salt

Heat the oil in a small pan over medium heat. Add the coriander, cumin, turmeric, cayenne, garam masala, and paprika. Cook for 3 minutes. Stir often. Cool completely.

In a large bowl, add the yogurt and the spice-oil mixture. Whisk. Add the lemon juice, garlic, salt, and ginger. Mix thoroughly.

Cut deep slashes in 3 to 4 places on the chicken legs. Coat the chicken in the marinade. Cover and chill for at least an hour but no more than 8 hours.

Preheat the oven to 425 degrees Fahrenheit.

Remove the chicken from the marinade. Bake on a baking sheet for 35 minutes. Chicken should be tender.

Serve with Indian flatbread.

Grilled Shrimp with Chile, Cilantro, and Lime

Serves 4

16 jumbo shrimp, unpeeled

6 Tbsp fish sauce, divided

4 Tbsp vegetable oil, divided, plus more for grill

2 tsp turmeric

32 cilantro sprigs, chopped

8 long red chilies, stemmed

10 garlic cloves

4 1-inch pieces ginger, peeled

¼ cup fresh lime juice

2 Tbsp light brown sugar

In a large bowl, add the shrimp, 2 tablespoons of fish sauce, 2 tablespoons of oil, and turmeric. Set aside for 30 minutes.

Add 4 tablespoons of fish sauce, 2 tablespoons oil, cilantro, and the remaining ingredients in a blender or food processor. Puree until a coarse mixture is formed. Transfer sauce to a small bowl. Set aside.

Build a medium-hot fire in a charcoal grill, or heat a gas grill to high. Shake excess liquid from shrimp and place shrimp on the grill. Cook for 6 minutes. Turn occasionally. Shrimp should be charred and cooked through.
Serve immediately with sauce.

Scorpio Shrimp

Serves 4

3 Tbsp olive oil

2 large onions, finely chopped

2 garlic cloves, finely chopped

¼ cup parsley, finely chopped

1 Tbsp dill, finely chopped

¼ tsp dry mustard

½ tsp sugar

2 14.5-oz cans diced tomatoes

½ cup tomato sauce

1 lb shrimp, peeled

1 cup Feta cheese, crumbled

Preheat oven to 425 degrees Fahrenheit.

Heat the oil in a frying pan. Add onion. Cook until onion is brown. Add garlic, parsley, and dill. Stir. Add the mustard and sugar. Stir. Add tomatoes and tomato sauce. Stir. Simmer for 30 minutes.

Add shrimp to the sauce. Cook for 4 minutes.

Pour mixture into a baking dish. Sprinkle with cheese. Bake for 15 minutes or until cheese melts.

Serve with rice.

Scalloped Oysters

Serves 4

1-pint fresh oysters
Juice of 1 lemon
2½ cups coarse cracker crumbs
1 stick butter
½ tsp salt
¼ tsp pepper
1 cup evaporated milk
¾ cup oyster liquor
1 tsp Worcestershire sauce

Preheat oven to 325 degrees Fahrenheit.

Lightly grease a 2 ½ quart casserole dish.
Drain liquor from oysters. Reserve ½ cup of the liquid.

Rinse oysters in cold water. Pick out any shell. Drain. Sprinkle the oysters with lemon juice.

Put the cracker crumbs into a large bowl. Add the salt, pepper, and melted butter to the cracker crumbs. Mix thoroughly.

Layer ½ of the cracker crumbs in the prepared casserole dish. Top with ½ of the oysters. Place another ½ of the crumbs on top of the oysters. Repeat with remaining oysters and crumbs.

In a medium bowl, add the milk, oyster liquor, and Worcestershire sauce. Pour slowly into casserole dish mixture.

Bake for 1 hour.

Scorpio Seafood Paella

Serves 12

1 tsp paprika

¼ cup extra-virgin olive oil

Salt

8 bone-in chicken thighs, with skin

4 6-oz sole fillets, halved lengthwise

2 pinches of saffron threads

4 cups vegetable stock, chicken stock or low-sodium broth

Freshly ground pepper

1 lb dry chorizo, sliced ¼ inch thick

8 small squids, bodies sliced crosswise into ¼ inch rings and tentacles halved

2 medium yellow onions, finely chopped

6 cloves garlic, minced

2½ cups Arborio or another short-grain rice

1 cup frozen peas

1½ lbs littleneck clams, scrubbed

1½ lbs mussels, scrubbed and debearded

1½ lbs lump crabmeat, well-drained and picked over

2 Tbsp chopped flat-leaf parsley

In a large bowl, add the paprika, 1 tablespoon of oil, and ¼ teaspoon of salt. Add the chicken. Toss. Cover and refrigerate for at least 3 hours or overnight.

In a shallow baking dish, arrange the sole in single layers. In a small bowl, add 1 tablespoon of the oil with 1 pinch of the saffron. Rub over the fish. Allow to stand at room temperature for 30 minutes.

In a saucepan, combine the vegetable stock with the remaining pinch of saffron. Add salt and pepper. Bring to a simmer. Cover and keep warm.

In a 14-inch paella pan or cast-iron skillet, heat the remaining 2 tablespoons of oil. Add the chicken and cook over moderately high heat for 15 minutes. Turn occasionally so chicken can brown on both sides. Transfer to a platter.

Add the chorizo to the pan. Cook for 3 to 4 minutes. Chorizo should be browned. Transfer the chorizo to the platter with the chicken. Pour off and reserve any excess fat in the pan. Allow a thin layer of fat to remain on the bottom of the pan for coating. Add the squid. Cook for 2 minutes. Squid should be white. Transfer the squid to the platter with the chicken.

Return 2 tablespoons of the reserved fat to the pan. Add the onion and garlic. Season with salt and pepper. Cook for 5 minutes. Stir occasionally, until translucent, about 5 minutes. Transfer the onion mixture to the platter.

Add 2 additional tablespoons of the reserved fat to the pan. Add the rice. Stir and cook over moderately high heat for 2 minutes. Add the chicken, chorizo, squid, and onion mixture to the pan along with any accumulated juices. Add the peas. Stir. Add the warmed stock into the pan. Cover and cook for 10 minutes.

Using tongs, nestle the clams and mussels into the rice. Cover and cook for 10 minutes.

Arrange the sole fillets and the crabmeat on the rice. Cover and cook for an additional 5 minutes. The sole should be cooked through and the rice should be tender. Remove the pan from the heat and let the paella stand for 5 minutes. Discard any mussels and clams that have not opened. Sprinkle the paella with the parsley. Serve immediately.

Cheese Soufflé

Serves 2 to 3

4 Tbsp butter

3 Tbsp grated Parmesan cheese

2 tsp flour

¾ cup milk

¾ cup grated Gruyere or Cheddar cheese

Pinch of cayenne pepper

Pinch of nutmeg

3 egg yolks

3 egg whites

¼ tsp salt

Preheat the oven to 375 degrees Fahrenheit.

Grease one 16-ounce or two 8-ounce ramekins with 1 tablespoon of butter. Coat with Parmesan cheese. Set aside.

Melt the remaining butter in a small saucepan over medium heat. Add the flour. Cook and stir for 1 minute. Add the milk. Cook and stir constantly until the sauce boils. Remove from heat. Stir in the cheese until it melts. Add the cayenne pepper and nutmeg. Stir. Add the egg yolks one at a time. Set aside.

In a second bowl, add the eggs and salt and beat until stiff peaks are formed. Stir ¼ of the egg whites into the cheese sauce so it loosens. Fold in the remaining egg whites. Spoon the mixture into the ramekins.

Bake for 40 minutes if using a 16-ounce ramekin. Bake for 20 minutes if using two 8-ounce ramekins.

Serve immediately.

Eggplant Parmesan

Serves 6

3 eggplants, peeled and thinly sliced

2 eggs, beaten

4½ cups Italian seasoned bread crumbs

6 cups spaghetti sauce, divided

16 oz Mozzarella cheese, shredded and divided

½ cup Parmesan cheese, grated, divided

Basil

Preheat oven to 350 degrees Fahrenheit.

In one bowl, add the eggs. Beat. In a second bowl, add the bread crumbs. Dip the eggplant slices in the eggs and then in the bread crumbs. Place the eggplant slices in a single layer on a baking sheet.

Dip the eggplant slices in egg, then in bread crumbs. Place in a single layer on a baking sheet. Bake for 5 minutes on each side.

Spread spaghetti sauce to cover the bottom of a 9 x 13-inch baking dish. Place a layer of eggplant slices in the sauce. Sprinkle with mozzarella and Parmesan cheeses. Repeat the layering ending with the cheeses. Sprinkle basil on top.

Bake for 35 minutes. The eggplant parmesan should be golden brown.

Saffron Fish and White Bean Soup

Serves 3 to 4

1 cup dry white beans

½ Tbsp olive oil

2 small onions, chopped

¾ tsp fennel seeds, crushed with a mortar and pestle

¼ tsp ground coriander

4 cloves garlic

4 sprigs fresh thyme

¼ tsp saffron threads

1 cup water

8 oz bottle clam juice

1 cup diced tomatoes including juices

½ tsp kosher salt

¾ lb of firm whitefish, into 2-inch pieces

Add two cups of water to a large pot. Soak and simmer the beans until they are soft. Drain the beans. Set aside. If using canned beans, drain and then rinse them.

Heat the olive oil in a large heavy pot over medium-high heat. Add the onion, fennel, coriander, garlic, and one thyme sprig. Cook for 5 minutes.

Crush the saffron threads with your fingers and add them to the pot. Pour in the water, clam juice, and tomatoes. Bring to a boil. Reduce heat to simmer. Cook for 5 minutes. Add the salt, fish, and beans. Let cook for an additional 5 minutes. The fish should be cooked through and flaky. Remove the sprigs of thyme.

Divide between two bowls. Removc leaves from the sprigs of thyme and sprinkle on top.

Crab Rangoon Salad

Serves 4

1 bunch asparagus, cut into 1-inch lengths

3 Tbsp water

¼ tsp salt

½ cup mayonnaise

3 green onions, finely chopped

3 Tbsp fresh lemon juice

1½ tsp honey

2 tsp low sodium soy sauce

8 oz crab meat, picked over

8 cups frisee lettuce, torn

1 cup rice crackers coarsely crushed.

In shallow 2-quart microwave-safe baking dish, add the asparagus and water. Add the salt. Cover with vented plastic wrap and microwave on high for 4 minutes. Drain well. Cool.

In a medium bowl, add the mayonnaise, green onions, lemon juice, honey, and soy sauce Whisk until smooth. Add the crab and asparagus. Toss to coat.

Divide lettuce among 4 serving plates. Top with crab mixture. Sprinkle with rice crackers.

Dark Chocolate Fudge

Makes about 12 pieces

3 cups semi-sweet chocolate chips

1 14-oz can sweetened condensed milk

¼ tsp salt

1½ tsp vanilla extract

1 cup nuts, chopped, optional

Line a 9 x 9-inch square pan with wax paper.

In a heavy saucepan, melt the chocolate chips, milk, and salt over low heat. Remove from heat and stir in the vanilla and walnuts, if using. Spread evenly into the prepared square pan.

Chill pan for 2 hours or until firm.

Turn fudge onto a cutting board. Peel off wax paper and cut into squares.

Store loosely covered at room temperature.

Plum Pudding with Hard Sauce

Serves 12

1 cup milk

3 cups soft bread crumbs

½ cup butter or margarine

½ cup molasses

½ cup raisins

½ cup currants

½ cup candied citron, finely chopped

2 tsp ground cinnamon

1 tsp baking soda

½ tsp salt

¼ tsp ground allspice

¼ tsp ground cloves

1 cup all-purpose flour

¾ cup butter or margarine

½ cup half-and-half

½ cup light corn syrup

1 cup packed brown sugar or granulated sugar

Fresh berries and orange peel, for garnish

Generously grease the bottom and side of a 4-cup heatproof mold. Put the bread crumbs in a large bowl. Pour in the half-and-half. Stir in ½ cup of butter or margarine and molasses. Mix well. Add the raisins, currants, citron, cinnamon, baking soda, salt, allspice, clove, and flour. Stir and blend well. Pour into the mold. Cover with foil.

Place mold on rack in Dutch oven. Pour in boiling water up to level of rack. Cover. Heat to boiling. Keep water boiling over low heat about 3 hours or until a toothpick inserted in center comes out clean. If adding water during steaming is necessary, uncover and quickly add boiling water.

For the hard sauce, add ¾ cup of butter or margarine, half and-half, corn syrup, and brown or granulated sugar in a 1½ quart saucepan. Mix well. Cook over low heat 5 minutes. Stir occasionally.

Unmold pudding, cut into slices. Serve warm with the hard sauce.

Garnish with fresh berries and orange peel.

Red Velvet Cupcakes

Makes 12 cupcakes

½ cup of granulated sugar

1 stick of butter, room temperature

2 eggs, room temperature

½ cups of cake flour

2 Tbsp of Dutch-processed cocoa powder

1 tsp baking soda

½ tsp baking powder

½ tsp salt

1 cup buttermilk

1 Tbsp red food coloring

½ tsp vanilla extract

1 tsp vinegar

Preheat the oven to 350 degrees Fahrenheit.

Add the butter and sugar to an electric mixer. Beat for 3 minutes on medium speed. The mixture should be light and fluffy.

Add the eggs, one at a time, to the electric mixer. Beat. Be sure to scrape down the sides of the bowl to ensure even mixing.

In a large bowl, sift together the cake flour, cocoa powder, baking soda, baking powder, and salt. In a second bowl, add the buttermilk, vinegar, vanilla extract, and red food coloring. Whisk.

In a third large bowl, add ¼ of the dry ingredients. Mix well. Add ⅓ of the wet. Continue adding in a dry, wet, dry pattern, ending with the dry ingredients.

Scoop into cupcake papers, about ½ or ¾ of the way full.

Bake for 18 to 22 minutes or until a toothpick comes out clean. Rotate the pan after the first 15 minutes of baking to ensure even baking. Allow to cool for one minute in the pan then transfer to a wire rack to cool completely.

Frosting

1 stick of butter, room temperature

8-oz package cream cheese, room temperature

3 cups of powdered sugar

1 tsp of vanilla extract

For the frosting, cream the butter and cream cheese together in a bowl. Scrape down the sides and bottom of the bowl to ensure even mixing. Add the vanilla extract. Mix well.

Add the powdered sugar. Taste continually to obtain the desired sweetness. Pipe onto the cooled cupcakes.

Sagittarius (November 22 – December 21)

The planet Jupiter rules Sagittarius. Jupiter is the planet of good luck and expansion. In ancient times, Jupiter was a very important Roman god. He was the ruler of the heavens.

The symbol associated with Sagittarius is the Archer. The Archer is a centaur. A centaur is a half man and half horse. It symbolizes man's attempt to free himself from his animal nature.

The color associated with Sagittarius is purple. Purple is the color of royalty. It also represents creativity and healing.

Sagittarius is a mutable fire sign. Mutable signs are adjustable and understanding. They are usually extroverts. Fire signs are zealous, ardent, freedom-loving people. Sagittarians are outgoing and independent. Their changeable natures make them comfortable in many different types of environments.

Sagittarius is a positive masculine sign.

Sagittarius rules the liver, hips, and thighs.

Because Jupiter rules Sagittarius, Sagittarians seem to be lucky. They appear to be at the right place at the right time, and so naturally, they are happy, cheerful people. Sagittarians are adventurous, brave, and wise like the centaurs in Greek mythology. Like all fire signs, Sagittarians are highly energetic and ambitious. Like all mutable signs, they are open to new ideas. However, because of the expansive influence of Jupiter, Sagittarians are restless, adventurous spirits with inquisitive natures. They like to travel and explore distant and exotic places. Sagittarians are also known as seekers. They seek truth and wisdom. They crave knowledge. These are the reasons why Sagittarians are referred to as the explorers and the philosophers in the zodiac.

The pointed arrow the centaur carries aims high. It represents the high ideals of the Sagittarian personality. Sagittarians have a strong character. They are honest, frank, and straightforward. Sagittarians are trustworthy. They are dependable and courteous. They are hospitable. Sagittarians are humanitarians. They volunteer to help people and animals. Sagittarians usually have a positive outlook on life.

Sagittarians are imaginative and talented. They usually have more than one interest. They are versatile and can do many things at one time. Sagittarians are good musicians, and often they are computer geeks. They are entertainers and good storytellers. Many Sagittarians are veterinarians because of their love of animals. Sagittarians like to roam the countryside because they like nature. Sometimes Sagittarians don't finish one project before they start another. It is because they can become bored rather quickly.

Because Jupiter is the planet of excess, Sagittarians are incredibly generous. At times, they can overindulge in their spending and be extravagant. They take chances because they believe in the luck of Jupiter. Sagittarians love their freedom which can make them highly independent. They have a difficult time forming habits, both good and bad. They also have a hard time committing to relationships and people. They can miss appointments and not finish projects. But overall, they are likable people. People usually excuse the Sagittarian person because they are so enjoyable to be around.

Overall, Sagittarians are very vigorous and healthy. They have a fluid movement that makes them graceful and coordinated. They are very good at sports and make good Olympians because they can compete very well on a higher scale. They like fierce competitiveness. Physically, Sagittarians are primarily tall and nicely built. They have long, well-shaped legs. They can be on the lean side because they are always on the go. Because Sagittarians love freedom, they like to be outdoors in the fresh air and sunshine. Exercise is a must for Sagittarians. They like to walk and bicycle ride. Sagittarians have extensive features and thick hair. They radiate charisma, and are often found smiling. Because of the luck of Jupiter, Sagittarians can live long, healthy lives with a minimum amount of care. More octogenarians are Sagittarians than any other zodiac sign.

Sagittarius represents high ideals, truth, and freedom. The dominant keywords for Sagittarius are "I SEE." Their dominant trait is optimism. Some famous Sagittarians are Woody Allen, Ludwig Van Beethoven, William F. Buckley, Dick Clark, Miley Cyrus, Sammy Davis Jr., Walt Disney, Kirk Douglas, Jamie Foxx, Jimi Hendrix, Bette Midler, Brad Pitt, Frank Sinatra, Britney Spears, and Mark Twain.

Sagittarians have a healthy appetite. They will eat almost everything because of their adventurous nature. They like hot and spicy foods with bold flavors because of their fiery nature. They have refined tastes and enjoy superb food and drink. Because Sagittarians love knowledge and travel, they will experience all the different types of cuisines throughout the world. Because Sagittarians are interested in many kinds of activities, they can take an interest in cooking and become quite good cooks. They are not like Cancers who prepare traditional meals for their families. Sagittarians would instead cook exotic dishes and try new recipes to entertain their friends.

Sagittarians tend to skip meals because they become so busy throughout the day. They should eat small meals and carry snacks in their backpacks throughout the day because it keeps them mentally and physically stimulated. Foods high in protein such as meats, poultry, fish, and cheese help sustain the Sagittarian energy level. Olives are an excellent food for Sagittarians because they permeate a high amount of energy into the body due to their fatty nature. They can give the Sagittarian an extra energy boost after they finish their intense exercise.

Sagittarians need to watch their liver, hips, and thighs. Beets have blood-cleansing properties which help safeguard the liver. Other foods good for the liver are tomatoes, dates, cherries, green beans, and corn. Apples are the perfect food for the outdoor, physically active Sagittarius. They help fight joint ailments because they aid in digestion and eliminate body toxins. Apples are also high in anti-oxidants and have natural sunscreen properties.

The mineral associated with Sagittarius is silica. It helps the nerves and connective brain tissue and helps prevent numbness in the limbs, fingers, and toes. Floppy hair, dull skin, and receding gums can occur if one is deficient in this mineral in the body. The skins of fruits, especially cherries, figs, lemons, oranges, pears, plums, prunes, and strawberries, contain silica. Raw salads and vegetables such as asparagus, cucumbers, Brussel sprouts, green peppers, and potatoes also contain silica. Eggs and yogurt are good food sources that also have silica.

The Archer does well when eating cinnamon and sage in their foods. Cinnamon is an anti-inflammatory that can help the joints. Since Sagittarians are known sometimes to indulge in candy, chocolate, butter, and creams, cinnamon is an excellent spice for them to eat because it helps keep blood sugar levels low. Sage is also an anti-inflammatory as well as an oxidant. Other herbs and spices suitable for the Sagittarian personality are basil, chervil, chicory, citron, clove, curry, garlic, ginseng, mint, parsley, and thyme.

For desserts, Sagittarians like tasty pastries. They also like sweet dishes with dried fruit and nuts. Blueberry muffins are considered a Sagittarian food. Being true to themselves, Sagittarians find excitement in new and different types of desserts.

Water and mineral water are excellent for Sagittarians to drink because they can get dehydrated with their intense exercise. They feel good when they drink water. Like their food, Sagittarians like exotic and different and new types of coffees and teas. Most likely, Sagittarians will drink wine because they like fine dining. They need to be careful of their alcoholic intake because of their liver.

Like Leos, one can always find a Sagittarius feasting at a banquet.

Sagittarius Food Guide

Fish

Anchovy
Bass
Bluefish
Carp
Catfish
Cod
Flounder
Grouper
Haddock
Halibut
Herring
Mackerel
Mahi-mahi
Monkfish
Ocean Perch
Orange Roughy
Red Snapper
Sablefish
Salmon
Sardine
Sea Bass
Shark
Smelt
Snapper
Sole
Sturgeon
Swordfish
Trout
Tuna
Turbot
Whitefish
Yellowtail

Seafood

Caviar
Clams
Crab
Crayfish
Lobster
Mussels
Octopus
Oysters
Scallops
Shrimp
Squid

Meat

Bacon
Beef
Lamb
Pork
Sausage
Steak
Veal
Venison

Poultry

Capon
Chicken
Cornish Game Hen
Duck
Goose
Pheasant
Quail
Turkey

Beans (High Carbohydrates)

Black-eyed Peas
Cannellini Beans
Chickpeas
Fava Beans
Garbanzo Beans
Great Northern Beans
Green Peas
Kidney
Lentils
Lima Beans
Navy Beans
Pinto Beans
Red Beans
Split Peas
White Beans

Grains/Breads/Cereals/Pastas

Amaranth
Barley
Bran
Brown Rice
Kamut
Millet
Oats
Pumpernickel
Spelt
Tabbouleh
Wheat

Whole-Grain Foods

Buckwheat
Rye

Cheese/Dairy Products

Butter
Cheeses
Cream
Eggs
Milk
Sour Cream
Yogurt

Oils

Coconut Oil
Fish Oil
Flax Seed Oil
Olive Oil
Peanut Oil
Safflower Oil
Sesame Oil
Vegetable Oil
Wheat Germ Oil

Vegetables

Alfalfa Sprouts
Artichokes
Arugula
Asparagus
Bean Sprouts
Beets
Beet Greens
Broccoli
Brussels Sprouts
Cabbage
Cauliflower
Carrots
Celery
Parsnip
Cucumbers
Dandelion Greens
Eggplant
Endive
Green Beans
Hops
Kale
Leeks
Lettuces
Mushrooms
Mustard Greens
Okra
Onions
Corn
Potatoes
Pumpkin
Radish
Spinach
Squash
Swiss Chard
Turnip
Turnip Greens
Wax Beans
White Beets
Yellow Beans
Zucchini
Collard Greens
Peppers

Fruit

Apples
Apricots
Avocados
Bananas
Blackberries
Blueberries
Boysenberries
Cherries
Coconut
Cranberries
Dates
Dried fruit
Figs
Grapes
Grapefruit
Lemon
Lime
Mandarins
Mango
Melons
Nectarines
Olives
Oranges
Papaya
Peaches
Pears
Plums
Pineapple
Pomegranate
Prunes
Raisins
Raspberries
Strawberries
Tangerines
Tomatoes

Herbs and Spices

Basil
Caraway
Cardamom
Cayenne
Chervil
Chicory
Chile pepper
Cinnamon
Citron
Clove
Coriander
Cumin
Curry
Garlic
Ginger
Ginseng
Marjoram
Mint
Mustard
Nutmeg
Oregano
Paprika
Parsley
Rosemary
Sage
Sweet Paprika
Tarragon
Thyme
Vanilla

Beverages

Coffee
Mineral Water
Red Wine
Water
White Wine
Tea

Other

Honey
Pecans
Sesame Seeds

Sagittarius Recipes

Sagittarians 'innate curiosity and love of experimentation make them excellent candidates for trying new cuisines, flavors, and combinations. They thrive on exotic, spicy, and uncommon dishes.

Apple Fritters

Makes 30

1 cup milk

1 egg, beaten

4 Tbsp butter or margarine

¼ cup sugar

¼ tsp salt

1 cup apples, chopped

3 cups flour

1½ tsp baking powder

1 tsp vanilla

¾ cup pecans, optional

Maple syrup

Melt the butter or margarine in a small saucepan over low heat.

Put the egg in a medium bowl. Beat. Add the milk and melted butter or margarine. Add the apples and vanilla.

In a large bowl, sift the flour, salt, and baking soda. Add the sugar and pecans, if using. Blend all the ingredients together. Add these dry ingredients to the milk mixture. Blend but do not over mix.

Heat the oil in a large skillet. Ensure that oil is very hot. Measure out a tablespoon of the fritter mixture and put it into the hot oil. Fry the fritters until they are a golden brown. Turn once so that both sides brown evenly. Cool.

Serve with maple syrup or with apple butter.

Moroccan Lamb Stew with Chickpeas and Apricots

Serves 8

3 lbs lamb stew meat, cubed

2 tsp ground coriander

2 tsp ground cumin

1 tsp ground ginger

3 tsp salt

½ tsp freshly ground pepper

4 Tbsp extra-virgin olive oil

1 large yellow onion, thinly sliced

1 Tbsp tomato paste

1 cup chicken broth

1 stick cinnamon

1 cup

1 canned chickpeas, rinsed and drained

1 cup dried, pitted apricots

4 medium carrots, halved lengthwise and cut into 1-inch chunks

1 12-oz package couscous

Preheat oven to 325 degrees Fahrenheit.

Place lamb on a large tray. Pat dry. In a small bowl, add the coriander, cumin, ginger, 2 teaspoons salt, and ½ teaspoon pepper. Mix well. Sprinkle over lamb on both sides.

Heat 2 tablespoons olive oil in a large ovenproof Dutch oven over medium-high heat. Place ¼ of lamb in pot in a single layer and cook for 7 minutes. Stir occasionally. Lamb should be golden brown. Transfer the lamb to a large bowl. Set aside. Repeat with the rest of the lamb. Add 1 tablespoon of olive oil for each batch.

Add onions to pot. Reduce heat to medium. Cook onions for 10 minutes. Stir often. Onions should be golden brown. Stir in tomato paste and cook for 2 minutes. Stir in broth. Scrap up any browned bits. Return lamb and its accumulated juices to pot. Add 2 cups water, cinnamon, and 1 teaspoon salt. Stir well and bring to a boil. Cover pot with lid. Cook in oven for 1 ½ hours.

Uncover pot. Stir in chickpeas, dried fruit, and carrots. Add more water if stew seems dry. Cover pot. Continue to cook for about 45 minutes. Lamb should be tender. If desired, uncover pot and cook for an additional 20 minutes. Stew will be thicker.

Approximately 15 minutes before serving, prepare the couscous according to package directions.

Remove stew from oven. Discard the cinnamon stick. Season with salt and pepper.

Ladle stew over couscous and serve.

Hungarian Beef Goulash

Serves 8

3 Tbsp butter

3 large onions, diced

2½ pounds beef stew, cut into 1-inch cubes

¼ tsp caraway seeds

¼ tsp dried marjoram

2 cloves garlic, minced

4 Tbsp paprika

¼ cup red wine

2 cups water

4 large white potatoes, peeled and cubed

Salt

Pepper

Sour cream, for garnish, optional

Melt the butter in a large pot over medium-high heat. Add the onions. Sauté the onions until they are soft. Add the meat. Brown the meat on both sides. Add the caraway seeds, marjoram, garlic, and paprika. Stir. Add the wine and water, Place heat on low and cook for 2½ hours.

Add the potatoes. Cook for an additional 45 minutes. Potatoes should be tender.

Add salt and pepper to taste. Garnish with sour cream when serving.

Indian Chicken

Serves 6 to 8

3-4 lbs chicken legs, thighs and/or wings

2 Tbsp peanut oil or melted butter

Salt

2 Tbsp sweet paprika

1 Tbsp cayenne pepper

3 tsp garlic powder

¾ tsp ground ginger

1 tsp ground cumin

1 tsp onion powder

1 tsp black pepper

1 tsp salt

½ tsp ground cardamom

¼ tsp ground cloves

Lemons or limes, for garnish

Preheat the oven to 325 degrees Fahrenheit.

Add the peanut oil or melted butter into a large bowl. Add the drumsticks and coat well. Add salt.

In a small bowl, add the sweet paprika, cayenne pepper, garlic powder, ginger, cumin, onion powder, pepper, salt, cardamom, and cloves.

In a large bowl, add half of the spice mix with the chicken. Place the chicken in a large casserole dish lined with aluminum foil. Add more spice mix over the chicken. Fold the aluminum foil to cover the chicken. Bake for 90 minutes.

After 90 minutes, open the aluminum foil. Continue to cook the chicken uncovered for an additional 15 to 20 minutes.

Baste the chicken with the sauce that forms at the bottom of the baking dish. Add lemon or lime juice. Garnish with lemons or limes.

Raspberry Balsamic Chicken

Serves 4

1 tsp vegetable oil
1 cup red onion, chopped
½ tsp dried thyme or 1 ½ tsp fresh thyme
½ tsp salt
4 boneless skinless chicken breasts
½ cup seedless raspberry preserves
2 Tbsp balsamic vinegar
¼ tsp black pepper

In a large nonstick skillet, heat oil over medium-high heat. Add the onion. Sauté for 5 minutes.

Add the thyme and ¼ teaspoon salt over the chicken. Add the chicken to the pan. Sauté each side for 7 minutes.

Remove the chicken from pan. Keep warm in oven.

Reduce the heat to medium. Add ¼ teaspoon salt, preserves, vinegar, and pepper to pan. Stir until the preserves melt.

Remove the chicken from the warm oven. Spoon the sauce over the chicken. Serve immediately.

Spanish Chicken

Serves 4

¼ cup olive oil
½ cup red wine vinegar
1½ tsp oregano, chopped
1 tsp salt
½ tsp garlic powder
¼ tsp pepper
4 bay leaves
¾ cup golden raisins
½ cup sliced or halved pitted green olives
3½ lbs chicken parts
2 Tbsp brown sugar
¾ cup dry white wine

In a medium bowl add the olive oil, vinegar, oregano, salt, garlic powder, pepper, bay leaves, raisins, and olives. Prick the chicken skin and add the marinade. Ensure the chicken is coated well. Cover. Refrigerate for 2 to 3 hours or overnight.

Preheat oven to 350 degrees Fahrenheit.

Place chicken parts in a 12 x 8 x 2-inch baking dish. Add the wine to the marinade. Pour over chicken. Add the brown sugar to the chicken.

Bake uncovered for 50 to 60 minutes. Chicken should be tender.

Remove bay leaves before serving.

Flounder with Dijon Mustard

Serves 4 to 6

1 lb of flounder fillets

4 tsp Dijon mustard

2 Tbsp salad dressing

3 Tbsp fresh chives, chopped

Cooking spray

Preheat the oven to 350 degrees Fahrenheit.

In a medium-sized bowl, add the mustard and salad dressing. Mix well. Add the chopped chives. Mix again.

Spray the dish with some cooking spray. Put the fish in a glass baking dish. Brush on the mustard mixture.

Bake fish for 13 to 15 minutes.

Vietnamese Mussels

Serves 4

2 lbs of mussels, cleaned and debearded

1 Tbsp of vegetable oil

1 yellow onion, chopped

Pinch of chili flakes

2 tsp of ginger, minced

1 Tbsp of curry powder

½ cup of chicken broth

1 13.5-oz can of coconut milk

Pinch of salt

1 stalk of lemongrass, chopped and smashed

Lime wedges, for garnish.

Put the mussels in a bowl of cold water and let them sit for about 10 minutes to ensure cleanliness. Drain the mussels and repeat the process. Discard any mussels that are open. They are dead and not good to eat. Debeard the mussels by pulling the threads. Place the mussels in a bowl of cold water.

Heat the oil in a large pan. Add the onion. Stir for 3 minutes. Onions should be soft and slightly translucent. Add the chili flakes, ginger, and curry powder. Stir for 1 minute.

Add the chicken broth and reduce by half. Add the coconut milk, salt, and lemongrass. Bring to a boil. Drain. Reduce heat to medium. Add the mussels. Cover and cook for 7 minutes. Mussels should open. Discard any mussels that are closed. They are dead.

Spoon the mussels and broth into bowls. Add lime juice. Garnish with lime wedge.

Italian Pizza with Feta Cheese

Serves 4 to 6

½ 12-inch pizza crust

3½ cups green bell peppers, chopped

1½ cups yellow onion, cut into rings

4 cloves garlic, crushed

2 Tbsp extra-virgin olive oil

1½ tsp dried Italian seasoning

¼ tsp salt

1 cup herbed Feta cheese, crumbled

Preheat oven to 450 degrees Fahrenheit.

Place the pizza crust on a pizza pan or a large, wide cookie sheet.

In a large bowl, add the peppers, onion, garlic, olive oil, Italian seasoning, and salt. Combine well. Spoon the mixture over the pizza crust. Top the pizza with the cheese.

Bake for 10 to 12 minutes. Pizza crust should be brown and the vegetables should be crispy and tender.

Slide the cooked pizza onto a pizza stone, large oval dish, or baking sheet. Use a pizza cutter to cut into slices.

Hawaiian Baked Beans

Serves 6

1 8-oz can pineapple slices, undrained

3 1-lb can pork and beans in tomato sauce

½ cup onions, chopped

2 Tbsp molasses

1½ tsp dry mustard

12 oz lunch meat

Whole cloves

2 tsp light brown sugar

Preheat oven to 350 degrees Fahrenheit.

Drain the pineapple slices from the can. Reserve the liquid. Slice the pineapple into halves.

Place the beans into a 1 ½-quart baking dish. Stir in the reserved pineapple liquid, onions, molasses, and mustard.

Cut the lunch meat into lengthwise quarters. Then cut each piece in half to make 8 strips. Stud each piece of meat with 2 or 3 cloves. Sprinkle with brown sugar. Arrange the meat on top of the beans alternately with the pineapple.

Cook for 30 minutes.

Middle Eastern Rice with Raisins

Serves 4

2 cups white rice, long grain

4 cups water

½ cup golden raisins

½ tsp salt

1 Tbsp cinnamon

¼ cup olive oil

Plain yogurt, optional

Wash the rice.

Put the rice in a large pot. Add the water. Stir. Add the raisins, salt, and cinnamon. Slowly pour the olive oil in the rice mixture. Mix with a spoon. Ensure that all ingredients are blended together.

Cook rice according to package directions. Stir the ingredients together after the rice is cooked. Spoon the rice onto a large platter. Serve with plain yogurt if desired.

Lentil Soup

Serves 6

1 Tbsp olive oil

1 celery stalk, diced

3 carrots, peeled and diced

1 large yellow onion, diced

4 garlic cloves, minced

Kosher salt

Freshly ground black pepper

1-quart vegetable broth

1 15-oz can diced tomatoes with juices

1½ cups lentils, rinsed

2 bay leaves

½ tsp finely chopped fresh thyme leaves

½ tsp freshly ground coriander

1½ tsp red wine vinegar or sherry vinegar

Bunch of spinach leaves

Sour cream, for garnish

Heat the oil in a large saucepan over medium heat for 3 minutes. Add and stir the celery, carrot, and onion into the saucepan. Cook for 10 minutes. The vegetables should be soft. Add and stir the garlic. Cook for 1 minute. Add several pinches of salt and fresh ground pepper.

Add the broth, tomatoes in their juices, lentils, bay leaf, thyme, and coriander. Stir. Cover and simmer for 15 minutes. Reduce the heat to low. Keep saucepan covered and continue simmering for an additional 15 minutes. The lentils and vegetables should be soft.

Add the vinegar. If needed, add more salt and pepper. Add the spinach. Stir until the spinach is wilted.

Pour the soup into bowls and garnish with a dollop of sour cream.

Greek Quinoa Salad

Serves 4 to 6

1 cup quinoa

2 cups water

1 small red onion, diced

1 small lemon

½ cup Kalamata olives, pitted and sliced

2 Tbsp extra-virgin olive oil

2 cucumbers, peels and diced

1½ cups cherry tomatoes, quartered

½ cup Feta cheese, crumbled

¼ tsp salt

¼ tsp pepper

Rinse the quinoa for about 2 to 3 minutes.

Fill a medium saucepan with water and salt. Add the quinoa. Bring to a boil. Reduce heat to low. Cover and simmer for 15 minutes. Remove the quinoa from the heat. Keep covered for an additional 5 minutes. After 5 minutes, fluff with a fork. Set aside in a large mixing bowl to cool down.

Dice the onion, olives, cucumbers, and tomatoes. Add the vegetable to the quinoa and squeeze lemon juice over it.

Slowly pour the olive oil over the quinoa. Add the feta, salt, and pepper. Toss well. If needed, add more lemon juice, salt, and pepper.

Oriental Salad

Serves 2 to 4

3 medium cucumbers

4 bell peppers, any color or any combination of colors

6 celery stalks

12 radishes

1 cup vegetable oil

4 Tbsp cider vinegar

2½ tsp sugar

1 tsp salt

Dash of pepper

2 Tbsp soy sauce

2½ tsp sesame seeds, toasted

Peel and slice cucumber into thin rounds. Clean and quarter the bell peppers. Slice the peppers lengthwise and cut into thin slices. Slice the celery and radishes into thin slices.

In a small bowl, add the oil, vinegar, sugar, salt, pepper, and soy sauce. Mix well. Cover and chill.

Mix the salad again before serving. Sprinkle with toasted sesame seeds.

Apple Cobbler

Serves 6

6 cups apples, peeled and sliced

1 cup sugar

2 Tbsp flour

½ tsp ground cinnamon

¼ tsp salt

¼ cup water

1 tsp vanilla extract

1 Tbsp butter or margarine, softened

½ cup flour

½ cup sugar

½ tsp baking powder

¼ tsp salt

2 Tbsp butter or margarine, softened

1 egg, slightly beaten

Preheat oven to 375 degrees Fahrenheit.

Lightly grease a 9 x 9-inch square baking pan.

In a large bowl, add the first 7 ingredients. Mix gently. Spoon the prepared mixture into the prepared baking pan. Dot with 1 tablespoon butter. Set aside.

Add the remaining ingredients to a large bowl. Spoon the apple mixture in the baking pan. This batter will spread during the baking process

Bake for 35 to 40 minutes.

Fig and Date Squares

Makes 18 to 20 squares

1 cup dried figs

1 cup dates, pitted

1 Tbsp lemon juice

1 Tbsp honey

1 cup pecans

¾ cup sweetened dried coconut, shredded

½ tsp cinnamon

About 10 to 12 extra dates, pitted

In a food processor or blender, add the figs, dates, lemon juice, and honey. Blend until the ingredients become a paste. May have to add a touch more of lemon juice and honey. Remove from processor or blender. Set aside.

Next add the pecans, coconut, and cinnamon to the food processor and blender. Blend until the ingredients become coarse crumbs. Add a few of the extra dates and keep adding until the crumbs hold together.

Press half of the crumbs into the bottom of an 8 x 8 glass container. Spread the fig/date paste over the crumbs. Take the remaining crumbs and spread over the paste. Press firm so that the paste and crumb compact together.

Blueberry Muffins

Makes 12 muffins

2 cups fresh blueberries, rinsed and cleaned

2 cups all-purpose flour

¾ cup granulated sugar

2 tsp baking powder

1 tsp baking powder

¼ tsp salt

Dash of nutmeg

1 cup whole milk

1 tsp pure vanilla extract

2 medium eggs

4 oz butter or shortening

Preheat oven to 400 degrees Fahrenheit.

Grease and flour a muffin pan. Another option is to insert paper muffin liners into the muffin pan.

In a large bowl, add the flour, baking powder, sugar, nutmeg, and salt.

Melt the butter or shortening in a small pan over low heat. Set aside to cool.

In a medium bowl, add the eggs. Beat. Add the milk and vanilla. Blend.

Pour a little bit of the melted butter into the egg-vanilla-milk mixture. Stir. Repeat until all the melted butter is incorporated well into the mixture.

Add the liquid ingredients to the dry ones. Mix for 5 or 6 seconds. The batter should be lumpy. Fold the blueberries into the batter by using a rubber spatula. Spoon the batter into the muffin pan.

Bake for 18 to 20 minutes. A toothpick inserted into the center of a muffin should come out clean.

Capricorn (December 22 – January 19)

Capricorn is ruled by the planet Saturn. Saturn is the Roman god that rules over the planting and reaping of grain.

The symbol associated with Capricorn is the Goat. The goat is shiny and surefooted. It climbs to great heights by taking advantage of every foothold in front of them.

The color associated with Capricorn is green. Green is the color of nature.

Capricorn is a cardinal earth sign. Cardinal signs are self-starters, and earth signs are pragmatic. Capricorns are ambitious and determined and are good at giving form to new ideas and projects.

Capricorn is a negative feminine sign.

Capricorn rules the bones, joints, and knees.

The Roman god Saturn is considered "top gun" because he was the father of many gods. He is known as a taskmaster. He taught his children discipline and the ethics of hard work. Capricorns are highly disciplined and responsible people. They are success-driven. They know they must work hard to be the "top gun" in their field of endeavor. Like all earth signs, Capricorns are practical and realistic. Like the goat, they take one step at a time to reach their goals. They are mature and blessed with common sense.

Like their father Saturn, Capricorns have a governing reputation. They are career-oriented, and they like to be leaders because they are geared towards power. Capricorns like honor and praise. They have a great sense of pride in themselves and their accomplishments. Sometimes this is seen by others as egotistical, but most often, their reserved nature makes them likable and popular with others. People usually have high regard for Capricorns and will easily relinquish power to them. Capricorns seize opportunities by using strategy instead of force. They are good at making decisions and handling crises.

Saturn is also known in astrology as "Father Time." Like the grand planter and reaper, he starts and finishes projects. Capricorns are good organizers because they know the value of time. They can plot out long-term goals that may take years to accomplish. Restriction, obstacles, and limitations are all aspects of Saturn. Capricorns will take all necessary steps to win out. Of all the signs of the zodiac, Capricorns are the most patient. They are willing to wait for rewards even if it takes a long time. Capricorns are cautious and, like any earth sign, conservative with money. They make good investments and gain wealth later in life.

Even though Capricorns are into reality, they are creative. They can put their dreams into action. People don't realize that they, too, need to enjoy the pleasures of life. People misinterpret their self-sufficiency as coolness. They are often perceived as aloof because they are so self-contained. Because Capricorns are good at organizing their life, they can often meddle in other people's lives and tell them what to do. Capricorns are looked at as the loner of the zodiac but they do cherish love and appreciation from others. Capricorns are sympathetic, caring, and can make great friends. They are not as gloomy as people think. They can have a dry sense of humor and wit. They are fun-loving. They tend to see things in black and white and don't much care for ambiguities. Like Sagittarians, they aim high. Unlike Sagittarians, they reach their goals methodically.

Capricorns are healthy people. They have good constitutions and are resistant to illnesses. It seems the longer they live, the healthier they become. Like Leos and Sagittarians, Capricorns are blessed with longevity. Physically, Capricorns are slender and are short to average height. They are stately-looking people. They have good bone structure. They are photogenic because they can have angular beauty in their facial structure. They have healthy teeth and serious-looking eyes. Their dress is one of practicality.

Capricorns are scholarly, but they know that exercise is important. They usually exercise in moderation. They like to walk because of its ease and practicality. Capricorns are hard workers outdoors because they like to be in nature. They make good gardeners and ground keepers. Capricorns can gravitate towards building and construction work.

Capricorn represents planning, fruition, and diligence. The dominant keywords for Capricorns are "I USE." Their dominant trait is steadiness. Some famous Capricorns are Humphrey Bogart, David Bowie, Kevin Costner, Katie Couric, Ellen DeGeneres, Benjamin Franklin, Stephen Hawking, Diane Keaton, Joan of Arc, Jude Law, Aristotle Onassis, Elvis Presley, Rod Stewart, Denzel

Washington, and Tiger Woods.

Capricorns do not have a strong appetite. They can have too much on their minds and get into a rut about food and eat the same things every day. Since they thrive on work, they usually will skip meals. They like simple and wholesome meals that are quick to prepare. Comfort foods like soups, stews, and meatloaf serve a Capricorn well. They will eat seasoned and spicy foods if it is made by someone else. They will not bother to do it for themselves. They are not gourmet cooks, and it is usually in the latter part of their life that they start to enjoy food. But even then, Capricorns avoid weight gain because they eat healthily.

Capricorn is the only sign that can eat whatever they desire. They like to eat what they grow. They often make fresh raw salads from arugula, beans, carrots, cucumbers, turnips, squash, and tomatoes grown from their garden. Beets, eggplant, avocado, melons, pineapples, and raisins are other foods. Capricorns need to remember to keep variety in their diet.

The mineral associated with Capricorn is calcium phosphate, and it helps in bone formation and bone health. For Capricorns to maintain their bones and teeth healthy, they must eat a diet high in protein and calcium, and they should eat a lean protein of fish, meat, or poultry every day. Dairy products such as eggs, cheese, buttermilk, and yogurt are excellent food choices for a Capricorn because of the calcium. Oranges, lemons, figs, celery, cabbage, kale, spinach, broccoli, corn, peas, potatoes, brown rice, whole wheat, almonds, and walnuts contain some foods calcium phosphate.

Capricorns prefer simple herbs like clove, basil, garlic, and parsley. Capricorns also like anise, cardamom, coriander, cumin, curry, fennel, ginger, licorice, mint, mustard, nutmeg, oregano, sweet pepper, sage, thyme, and vanilla.

Capricorns are drawn to comfort, simple, and substantial desserts. They like cakes, pies, and ice cream.

Sometimes Capricorn's skin tends to be dry and sensitive because Saturn holds sway over the spleen and gallbladder. Capricorns should ensure they drink plenty of water. Capricorns like hot coffee and iced tea. Wine is good for Capricorns because it helps their digestive system not get sluggish.

Even though Capricorns prefer simple food, they love dinners served with a beautiful tablecloth and the best china and silver.

Capricorn Food Guide

Fish

Anchovy
Bass
Bluefish
Carp
Catfish
Cod
Flounder
Grouper
Haddock
Halibut
Herring
Mackerel
Mahi-mahi
Monkfish
Ocean Perch
Orange Roughy
Red snapper
Sablefish
Salmon
Sardine
Sea Bass
Shark
Smelt
Snapper
Sole
Sturgeon
Swordfish
Trout
Tuna
Turbot
Whitefish
Yellowtail

Seafood

Caviar
Clams
Crab
Crayfish
Lobster
Mussels
Octopus
Oysters
Scallops
Shrimp
Squid

Meat

Bacon
Beef
Lamb
Pork
Sausage
Steak
Veal
Venison

Poultry

Capon
Chicken
Cornish Game Hen
Duck
Goose
Pheasant
Quail
Turkey

Beans (High Carbohydrates)

Black-eyed Peas
Cannellini Beans
Chickpeas
Fava Beans
Garbanzo Beans
Great Northern Beans
Green Peas
Kidney
Lentils
Lima Beans
Navy Beans
Pinto Beans
Red Beans
Split Peas
White Beans

Grains/Breads/Cereals/Pastas

Amaranth
Barley
Bran
Brown Rice
Kamut
Millet
Oats
Pumpernickel
Spelt
Tabbouleh
Wheat

Whole-Grain Foods

Buckwheat
Rye
Whole Wheat

Cheese/Dairy Products

Butter
Cheeses
Cream
Eggs
Milk
Sour Cream
Yogurt

Oils

Coconut Oil
Fish Oil
Flax Seed Oil
Olive Oil
Peanut Oil
Safflower Oil
Sesame Oil
Vegetable Oil
Wheat Germ Oil

Vegetables

Alfalfa Sprouts
Artichokes
Arugula
Asparagus
Bean Sprouts
Beets
Beet Greens
Broccoli
Brussels Sprouts
Cabbage
Cauliflower
Carrots
Celery
Collard Greens
Peppers
Cucumbers
Dandelion Greens
Eggplant
Endive
Green Beans
Hops
Kale
Leeks
Lettuces
Mushrooms
Mustard Greens
Okra
Onions
Parsnip
Potatoes
Pumpkin
Radish
Spinach
Squash
Swiss Chard
Turnip
Turnip Greens
Watercress
Wax Beans
White Beets
Yellow Beans
Zucchini
Corn

Fruit

Apples
Apricots
Avocados
Bananas
Blackberries
Blueberries
Boysenberries
Cherries
Coconut
Cranberries
Dried fruit
Peaches
Grapes
Grapefruit
Lemon
Lime
Mandarins
Mango
Melons
Nectarines
Olives
Oranges
Papaya
Pears
Plums
Pineapple
Pomegranate
Prunes
Raisins
Raspberries
Strawberries
Tangerines
Tomatoes
Figs

Herbs and Spices

Anise
Basil
Clove
Cardamom
Cinnamon
Coriander
Cumin
Curry
Fennel
Garlic
Ginger
Licorice
Mint
Mustard
Nutmeg
Oregano
Oregano
Paprika
Parsley
Sage
Sweet Pepper
Thyme
Vanilla

Beverages

Coffee
Red Wine
Water
White Wine
Tea

Other

Honey
Pecans
Sesame Seeds

Capricorn Food Recipes

Capricorns are more traditional when it comes to food, preferring homemade dishes. They care more about the quality of their meals than quantity, They're not usually into spicy foods, but they can be slightly heavy-handed with the salt.

Barbequed Meat Loaf

Serves 6 to 8

2 lbs hamburger

1½ cups bread crumbs

2 medium onions, chopped

1 green pepper, chopped

2 eggs

½ tsp salt

¼ tsp pepper

½ cup onion, chopped

2 Tbsp butter or margarine

2 Tbsp sugar

1 Tbsp dry mustard

⅔ cup water

1 Tbsp Worcestershire sauce

3 drops Tabasco sauce

½ tsp salt

¼ tsp pepper

¾ tsp paprika

¾ cup ketchup

1 Tbsp vinegar

Preheat oven to 350 degrees Fahrenheit.

To make the meat loaf, add the hamburger, bread crumbs, the two medium onions, green pepper, eggs, salt, and pepper into a large bowl. Mix well. Shape into a loaf. Put the loaf into a baking pan. The baking pan should be larger than the meat so the loaf doesn't touch the sides.

For the barbeque sauce, heat a large skillet over medium heat. Sauté the cup of onion in the butter for 3 minutes. Onion should be clear. Add the sugar, dry mustard, water, Worcestershire sauce, Tabasco sauce, salt, pepper, paprika, ketchup, and vinegar. Cook for 15 minutes. Pour this sauce over the meat loaf.

Bake for 1 hour.

Lamb Shanks with Swiss Chard

Serves 4

4 lamb shanks

2 tsp ground cinnamon, divided

1 tsp ground cardamom, divided

1 tsp salt

1 tsp freshly ground black pepper

2 Tbsp sunflower or olive oil

6 garlic cloves, minced

1 14.5-oz can diced tomatoes in juice

1¾ cups beef broth

1 Tbsp tomato paste

Pinch of ground cloves

1 lb Swiss chard, coarsely chopped

½ cup chopped flat-leaf parsley

In a small bowl, add half of the cinnamon, half of the cardamom, the salt, and pepper. Pat the lamb shanks dry. Season the shanks with the spice mixture.

Heat the oil in a large deep, heavy-bottomed pot over high heat. Add the lamb shanks and cook for about 5 minutes. Turn the shanks to ensure they are brown all over. Remove the shanks from the heat and set on a plate.

Reduce the heat to medium-low. Add the garlic and sauté for 2 minutes. Add the tomatoes in their juice, beef broth, tomato paste, the remaining cinnamon, and cardamom. Stir. Add the cloves. Increase the heat and bring to a boil. Scrape up the browned bits in the pot. Return the lamb shanks to the pot. Reduce the heat to a simmer. Cover and simmer for 1½ hours or until the lamb is tender.

Fifteen minutes before the end of cooking, add the Swiss chard. After 15 minutes of cooking, remove the Swiss chard with a slotted spoon and place in the center of a large platter. Place the lamb shanks over the Swiss chard.

Bring the cooking liquid to a fast boil. Reduce the heat and cook the liquid for about 10 minutes. The liquid should be thickened. Stir the parsley into the thickened sauce. Pour over the sauce over the platter.

Polish Stuffed Cabbage Rolls (Golabki)

Serves 8

1 cup water

½ cup white rice, uncooked

1 whole head of cabbage

1 lb lean ground beef

½ lb ground pork

½ cup onion, chopped

Small bag of carrots, shredded

1 egg, slightly beaten

¾ tsp salt

¼ tsp ground black pepper

1 10.75-oz can condensed tomato soup

In a medium saucepan, bring the cup of water to a boil. Add the rice. Stir. Reduce heat. Cover and simmer the rice for 20 minutes.

Remove the core from the head of cabbage. Place the whole head in a large pot filled with boiling, salted water. Cover and cook for about 2 to 4 minutes. Cabbage should be soft enough to pull out individual leaves. Drain.

In a medium mixing bowl, add the ground beef, ground pork, 1 cup of cooked rice, onion, shredded carrots, egg, salt, pepper, and 2 tablespoons of the tomato soup. Mix thoroughly.

Place the meat mixture on the individual cabbage leaves. Roll the leaves and secure them with toothpicks.

Place the cabbage rolls in a large skillet over medium heat. Pour the remaining tomato soup over the top. Cover and bring the rolls to a boil. Reduce heat to low. Simmer for 40 minutes. While simmering, stir and baste with the liquid occasionally.

Sloppy Joes

Serves 8

1 lb ground beef or ground turkey

1 onion, finely chopped

5 cloves garlic, minced

1 medium red bell pepper, seeded and finely diced

1¼ cups tomato sauce

2 Tbsp tomato paste

1 Tbsp red wine vinegar

1 Tbsp brown sugar

1 tsp dry mustard

½ tsp salt

¼ tsp black pepper

Add the meat and onion in a large nonstick skillet over medium-high heat. Cook for 5 to 10 minutes. The meat should be brown and cooked through.

Pour the pan drippings out of the pan to discard. Add the garlic and red pepper. Cook 5 to 10 minutes. The garlic and pepper should be tender. Add the tomato sauce, tomato paste, red wine vinegar, brown sugar, mustard, salt, and pepper. Reduce the heat to low. Cook at a simmer for 5 to 6 minutes. The Sloppy Joe mixture should be thickened.

Place about a ½ cup onto hamburger buns and serve.

Honey Chicken

Serves 6

6 chicken breasts, or one whole chicken, cut into parts

2 tablespoons olive oil

1 lemon, thinly sliced

Salt

Pepper

4 Tbsp honey

3 Tbsp sherry

¾ tsp cardamom seeds, ground

¾ tsp peppercorns, ground

Warm the honey in small saucepan over medium-low heat. Add the sherry, cardamom, and peppercorns. Stir well. Place the marinade and chicken in a large bowl. Coat the chicken with the marinade. Cover with plastic wrap. Let the chicken sit at room temperature for 30 minutes.

Preheat the oven to 350 degrees Fahrenheit.

Heat the olive oil in a large frying pan over medium-high heat. Place the chicken in the frying pan, skin side down. Sear the chicken until it is golden brown on both sides.

Put the lemon slices in a roasting pan. Put the chicken on top of the lemon slices. Brush the chicken with the marinade. Add salt and pepper.

Bake chicken breasts for 15 or 20 minutes. Bake chicken parts for 20 to 25 minutes.

Remove from oven and let chicken sit for 10 minutes before serving. Gravy can be made from the pan drippings.

Pan-Fried Fish Fillets

Serves 4

1 egg, beaten

1 lb fish fillets

½ cup milk

¾ cup flour

1 cup vegetable oil

¼ tsp salt

¼ tsp pepper

In a shallow dish, add the egg. Beat until blended. Add the milk to the egg. Stir. In a second shallow dish, add the four. Take each individual fish fillet and dip it into the egg mixture and then dip into the flour dish to coat.

Heat the oil in a large skillet over medium-high heat. When the oil is very hot, add the fish. Add the salt and pepper. Cook for 6 to 7 minutes. Fish should be golden brown and flake easily with a fork.

Tuna and Spinach Pasta

Serves 4

1 lb linguine

½ cup extra-virgin olive oil

4 garlic cloves, minced

2 6-oz cans tuna fish, packed in olive oil, drained

½ tsp salt

¼ tsp pepper

1 lb spinach

Cook the linguine according to package directions.

While the linguine cooks, heat the olive oil in a large skillet over medium-low heat. Add the garlic. Cook for 2 to 3 minutes. Garlic should be sizzling. Add the tuna, salt, and pepper. Stir. Keep warm over low heat.

Set aside 1 cup of boiling water from the linguini pot. Drain the pasta when it is done cooking. Place the cooked linguini back into its pot over moderate heat. Add the tuna mixture and the spinach to the pasta. Toss. Add some of the reserved pasta water to the pot.
Pour into bowls and serve immediately.

Macaroni and Cheese
Serves 4

4 cups milk

½ lb elbow Marconi

4 Tbsp butter

2½ cups Cheddar cheese, packed and grated

¼ tsp salt

¼ tsp pepper

½ cup bread crumbs

Preheat the oven to 400 degrees Fahrenheit.

Put the milk in a large saucepan over medium heat. Heat it until it becomes steamy. Add the macaroni. Bring to a boil. Reduce the heat to a simmer and cook for approximately 15 minutes. The macaroni should be cooked and it should absorb the milk.

Melt the butter in a separate saucepan over medium heat. Add the grated cheese, salt, and pepper. Stir. When the cheese melts, pour this sauce into the large saucepan containing the macaroni. Stir to ensure all the ingredients are combined well.

Place the macaroni with the cheese mixture into a baking dish. Sprinkle the top with breadcrumbs.

Bake for 20 minutes. The top should be lightly browned.

Vegetable Soup

Serves 12

1 32-oz container of vegetable stock
1 28-oz can crushed tomatoes
1 large onion, diced
5 stalks celery, diced
6 carrots, diced
1 head cabbage, shredded
1 14.5-oz can green beans
1 12-oz can yellow corn

½ tsp basil
½ tsp parsley
½ tsp garlic salt
½ tsp thyme
¼ tsp oregano
½ tsp salt
½ tsp pepper

In a large pot, over medium heat, add the vegetable stock, tomatoes, onion, celery, carrots, and cabbage. Stir. Add the basil, parsley, garlic salt, thyme, oregano, salt, and pepper. Simmer until the vegetables are tender. Add the green beans and yellow corn. Heat through. If needed, add more salt and pepper.

Vichyssoise (Potato and Leek Soup)

Serves 4 to 6

2 Tbsp butter or margarine
4 leeks, chopped
1 cup yellow onion
3 medium potatoes
2½ cups vegetable stock
½ cup milk
2 Tbsp butter or margarine
¼ tsp salt
¼ tsp freshly ground black pepper
Chives, minced, for garnish

In a large round pot, melt the butter or margarine over medium-high heat. Add the leeks, onion, and potatoes. Sauté for 3 minutes. Add 1 cup of the vegetable stock. Reduce heat to medium-low. Cover and cook for 15 minutes. Add more vegetable stock if needed. Add the milk, salt, and pepper. Simmer for 5 to 10 minutes.

Pour the soup into bowls. Garnish with chives. Serve hot or cold.

Ambrosia Salad

Serves 6 to 8

1 30-oz can fruit cocktail

1 16-oz can sliced peaches

1 16-oz can pineapple chunks

2 small cans mandarin orange sections

2 packages instant vanilla pudding mix

1 package shredded coconut

Drain the juice from all the fruit.

In a 2-quart casserole dish, add the fruit and 1 package of the vanilla pudding mix. Mix. Add ½ cup of the coconut. Mix. If not thick enough, add more vanilla pudding mix. Top with the remaining coconut.

Chill and serve.

Pecan and Goat Cheese Salad

Serves 8

4 oz whole pecans

1 Tbsp melted butter

1 Tbsp sugar

2 Tbsp honey mustard

3 clove garlic, minced

¼ cup balsamic vinegar

¾ cup olive oil

Salt

Pepper

1 lb mixed salad greens, including fresh baby spinach

4 oz Goat cheese

½ cup dried cranberries

1 red bell pepper, cored, seeded, and cut into ½ inch thin slices

Preheat oven to 300 degrees Fahrenheit.

Put the pecans into a small bowl. Add the melted butter to the pecans. Stir. Add the sugar. Mix well. Place the pecans in a single layer on a nonstick cookie sheet or you can use parchment paper to line cookie sheet.

Bake for 20 minutes. Cool.

In a medium-size bowl, add the honey mustard, garlic, and balsamic vinegar. Whisk together. Slowly pour the oil into the mixture. Whisk. Add salt and pepper to taste.

In a large bowl, add the salad greens and baby spinach. Add the Goat cheese, dried cranberries, red bell pepper, and pecans. Toss with ¼ cup of the dressing.

Serve immediately. Chill remaining dressing.

Dark Chocolate Pudding

Serves 4

½ cup granulated sugar

3 Tbsp cornstarch, sifted

¼ cup cocoa powder, sifted

¼ tsp salt

1 cup fat-free half and half

1 cup milk

2 oz chopped unsweetened dark chocolate

½ tsp vanilla extract

Whipped cream, for garnish

Dark chocolate, chopped, for garnish, optional

Add the sugar, cornstarch, cocoa powder, and salt in a small saucepan. Whisk. Slowly add the half and half and milk to prevent lumps. Whisk. Heat the mixture over medium-high heat. Whisk until the mixture steams. Add the chopped dark chocolate. Stir until it has melted and the pudding has bubbled and thickened. Remove from heat. Add the vanilla extract. Stir.

Pour the pudding into 4 separate serving dishes. Place plastic wrap directly onto pudding and refrigerate for 2 hours. The pudding should be completely chilled. Remove the plastic wrap from the pudding serving dishes. Garnish the pudding the whipped cream and the dark chocolate, if using.

Pumpkin Pie

Serves 8

1 9 inch pie shell, unbaked

1 cup sugar

1 tsp cinnamon

¼ tsp salt

¼ tsp ground ginger

¼ tsp ground cloves

2 large eggs

2 cups pumpkin

1 12-oz can evaporated milk

Preheat oven to 350 degrees Fahrenheit.

Put all of the ingredients into a blender or food processor. Blend on medium speed. Ensure all ingredients are evenly mixed. Pour into the pie shell.

Place the pie shell with the ingredients on a large cookie sheet. Bake for 45 to 50 minutes.

Serve with whipped cream or ice cream.

Aquarius (January 20 – February 18)

Aquarius is ruled by the planet Uranus. Uranus is the planet of sudden and unexpected change, and it was the first modern planet to be discovered in 1781.

The symbol associated with Aquarius is the water bearer. Water flows freely out to the world.

The color associated with Aquarius is blue. Blue is the color of the sky.

Aquarius is a fixed air sign, and they do not move easily. On the other hand, air signs are flexible. Aquarius is a sign of paradoxes. As an air sign, Aquarians are intellectually oriented. As a fixed sign, they are persistent in their goals and commitments.

Aquarius is a positive masculine sign.

Aquarius rules the circulatory system, shins, and ankles.

Because Uranus is considered a modern planet, Aquarians are futuristic and visionary. They are original, unorthodox, and avant-garde in their thinking. Because Uranus is the planet of the unconventional, Aquarians are inventive. They like modern science and music composition. Aquarians are liberal and progressive in their social and political views. They are excellent at promoting new and different ideas. They follow no one but themselves. Aquarians are often thought of as geniuses. Yet, as flowing as Aquarians seem to be, they can become quite fixated in their opinions. They have strong likes and dislikes, and they don't like to compromise.

In astrology, the Water Bearer brings water as a gift to the world. The water showers the world freely and equally. Aquarians shower the world with their gifts of thoughts and new ideas. For this reason, Aquarians are great humanitarians of the world. They are concerned with larger-than-life situations and have visions of making the world a better place to live. They think about ideal living situations. They are not so worried about day-to-day tasks and responsibilities. They would instead leave that to someone else like a Capricorn.

Because Aquarians are objective and intellectually oriented, they can come across as being aloof, detached, and uncaring in their dealings with people on an emotional level. However, Aquarians are friendly and people-oriented. They are outgoing and usually attract many different types of people as friends. Aquarians are polite, and they listen when people talk. They are genuinely interested in people and want to know what makes them tick. Aquarians are nonjudgmental and believe that everyone has the right to be themselves. Even though Aquarians love their independence, they do make loyal friends. Aquarians are kind and sensitive, and their feelings can get hurt by an insensitive remark.

Being an air sign, Aquarians are quick learners. They can conceptualize and idealize quite quickly. They tend to know a lot about everything. Because of their independent streak, Aquarians usually work for themselves. They are hard workers, and their wide range of different skills helps them in their entrepreneurial pursuits. Aquarians have abundant energy, and they like to nourish their minds. For these reasons, Aquarians can have more than one business or job. Aquarians are the types of people who can stay up all night. Like all air signs, Aquarians are communicators, and the message they like to convey to the world is one of love.

Aquarians have strong bodies and good coordination. Physically, they are tall and slim. They have nice facial traits and expressions. They can be serious-looking. They tend to have thick hair. Because Uranus rules the lower extremities, Aquarians usually have well-shaped legs and slender ankles. Aquarians can be creative and eccentric in their dress. In any case, their appearance gives the impression of originality. Being an Air sign, Aquarians are mobile, and they don't mind exercises like walking or bike riding. They need to feel the air against their face. Aquarians like yoga because it has spiritual healing associated with it. Aquarians usually exercise in moderation because they are more mentally active than physically active. Aquarians don't like cold weather because of their sensitive circulatory system. One would not find them doing winter sports.

Aquarius represents hopes, dreams, and wishes. The dominant keywords for Aquarius are "I KNOW." Their dominant trait is friendliness. Some famous Aquarians are Lewis Carroll, Geena Davis, James Dean, Neil Diamond, Charles Dickens, Clark Gable, John Grisham, Alicia Keys, Abraham Lincoln, Paul Newman, Yoko Ono, Franklin Delano Roosevelt, Justin Timberlake, John Travolta, and Oprah Winfrey.

Aquarians are not interested in food that much because they are off saving the world. Even though their non-eating lifestyle can keep them slim, it allows little time for balanced meals. Aquarians like food snacks and can easily eat the wrong types of food. Aquarians need to eat correctly to maintain their energy and keep their ideal weight. More than any other sign, Aquarian's health will take an unexpected turn for the worse and then, just as fast, reverse again. Aquarians eat in cycles. They can crave exotic and foreign cuisines due to their nonconformist nature and then shift to simple and light meals and eat the same food for weeks.

Aquarians should eat foods that stimulate blood circulation. They need to keep their blood pressure and blood sugar levels even. Aquarians need to limit fat and sugar in their diet. They need high protein foods and fresh fruits and vegetables. Lean meats, poultry, and fresh fish are healthy protein foods for Aquarians. Beets, broccoli, carrots, peppers, tomatoes, pineapple, pomegranates, figs, and dates are excellent fruits and vegetables for Aquarians. Other excellent food choices for Aquarians are brown rice, buckwheat, whole wheat, wheat germ, yogurt, and natural cheeses. Varicose veins can be a problem for Aquarians, so they should eat foods high in Vitamin C to keep their legs healthy. Brussels sprouts, cauliflower, kale, sweet potatoes, kiwi, melons, and papaya contain high levels of Vitamin. C. Aquarians tend to like lemons and sour cherries, two foods that also contain high levels of Vitamin C

Aquarians need brain food for their genius-like minds. They tend to overthink and over strategize their ideas and concepts. Aquarians can suffer from bad nerves and nervous disorders such as stress and anxiety that may result from their intense mental activity. Foods that are excellent for the brain and the nervous system are fish, avocado, bananas, blueberries, blackberries, raspberries, strawberries, all types of nuts, and milk. Eggs can help the brain, and asparagus, legumes, and mushrooms help aid the nervous system.

The mineral associated with Aquarius is sodium chloride, also known as table salt. A lack of sodium chloride in the blood system can cause dehydration. Foods high in sodium chloride are ocean fish, lobster, tuna, clams, oysters, spinach, radishes, celery, cabbage, lettuce, squash, lentils, apples, peaches, pears, lemons, oranges, almonds, pecans, and walnuts.

Aquarians usually appreciate the different flavors herbs and spices can bring to various kinds of food. They especially like the Chinese herb star anise. Basil is an excellent herb for Aquarians because it promotes blood circulation and is suitable for the brain. Clove, ginger, and rosemary are also ideal for Aquarians because they promote good blood circulation. Marjoram, mint, and peppermint help prevent anxiety, and sage is good for the brain. Other herbs and spices that are good for Aquarians are cumin, garlic, lemongrass, lemon pepper, licorice, and parsley.

Aquarians love coffee. They often make it a meal. They are better to drink caffeine-free coffee because of their sensitive nervous systems. Herbal teas are an excellent choice for Aquarians because of their calming effect. Aquarians are known to like champagne and beer. They should not drink too much alcohol because it is not suitable for the nervous system. The best beverage Aquarians should drink is well-oxygenated water

Aquarians should not overdo it with sweets because of their sensitive systems. Even though sugar can play havoc on the nerves, dark chocolate has a calming effect.

Aquarians like informal dinner gatherings. They like shining sparkly crystals on the table.

Aquarian Food Guide

Fish

Anchovy
Bass
Bluefish
Carp
Catfish
Cod
Flounder
Grouper
Haddock
Halibut
Herring
Mackerel
Mahi-mahi
Monkfish
Ocean Perch
Orange Roughy
Red Snapper
Sablefish
Salmon
Sardine
Sea Bass
Shark
Smelt
Snapper
Sole
Sturgeon
Swordfish
Trout
Tuna
Turbot
Whitefish
Yellowtail

Seafood

Caviar
Clams
Crab
Crayfish
Lobster
Mussels
Octopus
Oysters
Scallops
Shrimp
Squid

Meat

Lean Red Meats
Veal
Venison

Poultry

Capon
Chicken
Cornish Game Hen
Duck
Goose
Pheasant
Quail
Turkey

Beans (High Carbohydrates)

Black-eyed Peas
Cannellini Beans
Chickpeas
Fava Beans
Garbanzo Beans
Great Northern Beans
Green Peas
Kidney
Lentils
Lima Beans
Navy Beans
Pinto Beans
Red Beans
Split Peas
White Beans

Grains/Breads/Cereals/Pastas

Amaranth
Barley
Bran
Brown Rice
Millet
Oats
Pumpernickel
Rye
Wheat
Wheat Germ

Whole-Grain foods

Buckwheat
Kamut
Spelt
Tabbouleh
Whole Wheat

Cheese/Dairy Products

Butter
Cheeses (low fat)
Cream (low fat)
Eggs
Milk (low fat)
Sour Cream (low fat)
Yogurt (low fat)

Oils

Coconut Oil
Fish Oil
Flax Seed Oil
Olive Oil
Peanut Oil
Safflower Oil
Sesame Oil
Vegetable Oil
Wheat Germ Oil

Vegetables

Alfalfa Sprouts
Artichokes
Arugula
Asparagus
Bean Sprouts
Beets
Beet Greens
Broccoli
Brussels Sprouts
Cabbage
Cauliflower
Carrots
Celery
Collard Greens
Corn
Cucumbers
Dandelion Greens
Eggplant
Endive
Green Beans
Hops
Kale
Leeks
Lettuces
Mushrooms
Mustard Greens
Okra
Onions
Parsnip
Peppers
Potatoes
Pumpkin
Radish
Spinach
Squash
Swiss Chard
Turnip
Turnip Greens
Watercress
Wax Beans
White Beets
Yellow Beans
Zucchini

Fruit

Apples
Apricots
Avocados
Bananas
Blackberries
Blueberries
Boysenberries
Cherries
Coconut
Cranberries
Dates
Dried fruit
Figs
Grapes
Grapefruit
Kiwi
Lemon
Lime
Mandarins
Mango
Melons
Nectarines
Olives
Oranges
Papaya
Peaches
Pears
Plums
Pineapple
Pomegranate
Prunes
Raisins
Raspberries
Strawberries
Tangerines
Tomatoes

Herbs and Spices

Anise
Basil
Cardamom
Cayenne
Chile Pepper
Cinnamon
Clove
Cumin
Curry
Dill
Fennel
Garlic
Ginger
Lemongrass
Lemon pepper
Licorice
Marjoram
Mint
Nutmeg
Paprika
Parsley
Peppermint
Rosemary
Sage
Thyme
Vanilla

Beverages

Beer
Champagne
Decaffeinated Coffee
Decaffeinated Herbal tea
Oxygenated Water
Red Wine
White Wine

Other

All Kinds of Nuts
Honey

Aquarius Food Recipes

Aquarians need high protein and low-calorie foods to sustain them though out the day so they can keep up their creativity. These people are vegetarians and love the taste of fruits and vegetables more than protein-rich food.

Light N' Fluffy Pancakes

Serves 10 to 12

1 cup flour

2 Tbsp baking powder

2 Tbsp sugar

Pinch of salt

1 egg, beaten

1 Tbsp oil

1 cup milk

In a large bowl, add the flour, baking powder, sugar, and salt. Mix together.

In a second bowl, add the egg, oil, and milk. Add these liquid ingredients to the large bowl of dry ingredients. Mix well.

Heat a lightly oiled griddle or skillet over medium-high heat. Pour about ¼ cup of the batter onto the griddle or skillet for each individual pancake. Cook until the pancakes are brown on both sides.

Put the oven on warm to keep the pancakes hot while the rest of the batter is being cooked.

When done cooking, add butter and syrup and serve hot.

Beef and Broccoli

Serves 4

1 lb round steak, sliced in thin strips

2 cloves garlic, minced

1 cup chopped onion

1 can beef broth

2 Tbsp cornstarch
1 Tbsp brown sugar
2 Tbsp soy sauce
½ tsp garlic powder
¼ tsp ground ginger
4 cups broccoli florets
4 cups cooked rice

Add cooking spray to a large skillet and heat over medium heat for one minute.

Add the beef strips, garlic, and onion. Stir fry until brown. Move the beef to a plate and keep warm in the oven.

Add the beef broth and broccoli florets to the skillet. Cover and simmer for 15 minutes. Broccoli should be tender-crisp. Add the cornstarch, brown sugar, garlic powder, ginger, and soy sauce. Cook until the mixture begins to thicken. Stir constantly. Return the beef to the skillet. Heat through. Stir and mix well.

Serve over rice.

Lemon and Thyme Chicken

Serves 4

3 Tbsp flour
¼ tsp salt
¼ tsp pepper
1 lb boneless skinless chicken breast halves
2 tsp olive oil
1 yellow onion, chopped
1 Tbsp butter
¾ tsp dried thyme
1 cup chicken broth
3 Tbsp lemon juice
Fresh parsley, minced, for garnish

In a small bowl, add the flour, salt, and pepper. Stir to blend. Measure out 4 ½ teaspoons of this mixture and reserve. Spread the remaining flour mixture all over the chicken.

Coat a large nonstick skillet with cooking spray. Add the oil and chicken. Cook over medium for 8 minutes on each side. The juices should run clear. Remove. Keep chicken warm in the oven.

In the same skillet, add the onion. Sauté for 3 to 4 minutes. Onions should be tender. Add the thyme and the reserved flour mixture. Stir. Add the broth and lemon juice. Stir. Scrape up the browned bits from the bottom of the pan. Bring to a boil. Stir. Cook for 2 to 3 minutes. Sauce should be thickened. Serve over chicken. Garnish with parsley.

Scallops in White Wine

Serves 4

1 Tbsp olive oil
½ cup shallots, minced
1 lb bay scallops
1 cup dry white wine
1 Tbsp fresh lemon juice
¼ tsp salt
¼ tsp pepper

Heat the olive oil in a large skillet over medium-high heat. Add the shallots. Sauté for 2 minutes. Shallots should be lightly browned. Add the scallops. Sauté for only 30 seconds. Add the white wine. Cover and cook for 3 minutes. Scallops should be opaque. Remove the scallops from the skillet with a slotted spoon.

Add the lemon juice, salt, and pepper to the wine mixture. Simmer for 2 minutes. The sauce should be diminished.

Return the scallops to the wine mixture. Cook for a few minutes. Scallops just need to be heated through.

Festive Beets

Serves 6 to 8

2 14.5-cans red beets, drained

¾ cup sugar

1 Tbsp cornstarch

½ tsp salt

½ cup vinegar

2 Tbsp orange marmalade

2 Tbsp butter or margarine

In a large saucepan, add the sugar, cornstarch, salt, and vinegar over medium heat. Cook until the ingredients are thickened. Add the marmalade and butter. Blend. Change the heat to low. Add the beets. Cook for 10 minutes. Stir occasionally.

Spinach Pastry

Serves 4

1 10-oz package frozen chopped spinach

1 Tbsp greens onions, minced

3 eggs, beaten

2 Tbsp butter or margarine

¾ cup sour cream

1½ cups Parmesan cheese

1 Tbsp flour

Pinch of nutmeg

¼ tsp salt

¼ tsp black pepper

Preheat oven to 350 degrees Fahrenheit.

Butter a 1-quart casserole or soufflé dish.

Cook spinach according to package directions. As the spinach is cooking, add the green onions. Drain. Add the eggs and sour cream. Blend. Add the Parmesan cheese and flour. Blend. Add the butter, nutmeg, salt, and pepper. Stir. Pour into the prepared casserole or soufflé dish.

Cook for 25 to 30 minutes. The center should be set.

Sweet Potato Soufflé

Serves 8

2 cups sweet potatoes, cooked and mashed

½ cup sugar

2 eggs

1 tsp salt

3 Tbsp butter or margarine

1 cup milk

1 tsp nutmeg

2 tsp vanilla

½ cup raisins

Marshmallows

½ cup walnuts or pecans, chopped

Preheat oven to 325 degrees Fahrenheit.

Grease a 1½-quart casserole dish.

Peel the potatoes. Cook the potatoes in a large saucepan until they are tender. Mash the potatoes. Add the sugar, eggs, salt, butter or margarine, milk, nutmeg, and vanilla to the mashed potatoes. Mix well.

Place the potatoes in the prepared casserole dish. Cook for 35 to 40 minutes. The casserole should be firm. Place the marshmallows and nuts on top. Return to the oven for 5 minutes until brown on top.

Cranberry Salad

Serves 6 to 8

1 quart cranberries, ground

1 orange, ground

2 cups sugar

2 packages lemon gelatin

1 cup hot water

1 cup cold water

Dissolve the 2 packages of lemon gelatin in 1 cup of water. Then, add 1 cup cold water to the lemon gelatin.

In a large bowl, add the lemon gelatin with the ground cranberries, ground orange, and sugar. Mix well. Pour into a mold. Refrigerate to set.

Fresh Fruit Salad

Serves 4 to 6

1 cup vanilla yogurt

2 Tbsp honey

¼ tsp ground cinnamon

2 large oranges, seedless, peeled, sliced, and halved
½ pineapple, peeled, cored, sliced, and cut into wedges
1 apple, cored and chopped
1 pear, cored and sliced into wedges
1 kiwi fruit, peeled and sliced

In a small bowl, add the yogurt, honey, and cinnamon. Blend well.

Nicely arrange the fruit on plates.

Pour the honey-yogurt dressing on top.

Cherry Delight

Serves 12

1 angel food cake

2 cups milk

8-oz container sour cream

1 large vanilla instant pudding mix

1 cup cherry pie filling

Whipped cream, optional

Break the angel food cake into small pieces and place in an 8 x 12 inch dish.

In a medium bowl, add the milk, sour cream, and the instant pudding mix. Pour this mixture evenly over the angel food cake pieces. Cover and refrigerate several hours or overnight.

Add the cherry pie filling to the angel food cake mixture.

Chill.

Serve as is or with whipped cream.

Devil's Food Cake

Makes 1 cake

2 sticks butter or margarine

1¼ cups sugar

½ tsp salt

1 tsp baking soda

2 tsp vanilla

3 Tbsp cocoa

2 cups flour

1 cup water

3 eggs

1 cup sugar

½ stick butter or margarine

¼ cup cocoa

½ cup milk

Preheat oven to 350 degrees Fahrenheit.

In a large bowl, add the butter or margarine and sugar. Cream together. Add the salt, baking soda, vanilla, and cocoa. Mix well. Add the eggs. Blend. Add the flour and water. Mix together. Pour into 9 x 13 inch baking pan.

Bake for 25 minutes.

For the icing, add the sugar, butter or margarine, cocoa, and milk to a medium saucepan. Mix together and bring to a boil. Boil for 1 minute. Cool for 5 minutes before putting on cake.

Ice Cream Pie

Serves 6

1 small vanilla instant pudding

1 cup milk

2 cups coffee ice cream, softened

1 pie crust, baked

Add the pudding mix and milk into a large bowl. Beat. Add the ice cream. Stir and mix well. Pour in the baked pie crust.

Refrigerate 1 hour or more.

Quick Lemon Cookies

Makes 20 to 24 cookies

1 box lemon cake mix

1 egg

1 cup cool whip

1 Tbsp lemon juice

Sugar

Preheat oven to 350 degrees Fahrenheit.

Place some sugar in a bowl.

In a second bowl, add cake mix, egg, cool whip, and lemon juice. Mix well. Roll the dough into small balls. Roll the balls of dough is some sugar.

Place the dough balls 1 inch apart on a large cookie sheet. The cookies will flatten out and spread as they bake.

Bake for 8 to 10 minutes.

Pisces (February 19 – March 20)

The planet Neptune rules Pisces. Neptune is the ancient god of the sea, and it is the planet of illusion and mystery. It was the second of the modern planets to be discovered in 1946.

The symbol associated with Pisces is two fish tied to each other swimming in opposite directions. They represent the dual nature of life, representing the consciousness and the unconscious.

The color associated with Pisces is light green and turquoise, which are the sea's colors.

Pisces is a mutable water sign. Mutable signs are versatile and receptive, and water signs are mystical and caring people. Pisces people have a malleable nature, and they are patient, gentle, and kind.

Pisces is a negative feminine sign.

Pisces rules the feet.

Like all water signs, Pisceans are emotional, sensitive, intuitive, and secretive. Pisceans, however, take things a little bit further. Pisces is the last sign of the zodiac. It is the end of the cycle, and it signifies eternity, spiritual rebirth, and even reincarnation. People born under the sign of Pisces are on a high spiritual plane. They have an otherworldly quality about themselves Many Pisceans are psychics. They have the gift of prophecy and clairvoyance. They are pulled between the material and spiritual world. The two fish, a representative of Pisces, signify hidden depths. Pisces people can be bohemian-like.

Because Neptune rules Pisces, Pisceans can be elusive and unpredictable. As the last of the twelve zodiac signs, Pisces people have a personality that combines all the signs. It is why Pisceans have many different sides and moods and why they are so changeable. More than any other signs, Pisceans can quickly adapt to people and their surroundings. They are the chameleons of the zodiac because they are so receptive to their environment and the needs of others. They can take on another person's worries or joys as their own.

Pisceans are known as the "dreamers" of the zodiac, even though their dreams can be vague and impractical. Pisces people are idealists. They can rework their ideals if necessary because they are broad-minded and mutable. Pisceans are imaginative, romantic, and sentimental. They are the most creative of all the zodiac signs. They are devoted to fantasy, art, and drama. Pisceans make good poets, writers, and musicians. Being dreamers, Pisceans can sometimes be impractical and procrastinators. Sometimes Pisces people are looked on as lazy because they lack discipline. Because Pisces people are shy and unaggressive, they are seen as not having a backbone. However, Pisces people are capable of hard work and will sacrifice greatly for a cause. They are also intellectually curious.

Pisces people are very charming, and they are usually quite popular. They can be mischievous, and they love to laugh. They make a loyal and unselfish friend. They are charitable and generous and are willing to help anyone who needs it. They see the inner essence of a person. They are not concerned with what is seen on the surface. Pisces people have many interests, and they are skilled at various things. They learn by absorption rather than logic. Pisceans achieve their high intellectual capability through their sensitivity and instinct. Pisceans will sacrifice greatly for a friend. They have a unique power. Pisceans are not often looked at as leaders because of their soft, introverted nature. They are perceived as guides, teachers, or role models.

Pisceans have delicate constitutions due to their sensitive and emotional personalities. Illness is often emotionally based for the Pisces person. Physically, Pisces people are often short to average height and can be rounded or plump. They usually have large, beautiful eyes, soft hair, and beautifully shaped feet. Pisces people tend to have low energy. Being the fish though, Pisces people do like water sports, and they make good swimmers. Many Pisceans are excellent dancers because of their nimble feet.

Pisces represent understanding, love, and make-believe. The dominant keywords for Pisces are "I BELIEVE." Their dominant trait is compassion. Some famous Pisces are Drew Barrymore, Michael Caine, Johnny Cash, Glenn Close, Billy Crystal, Albert Einstein, George Harrison, Ron Howard, Steve Jobs, Jon Bon Jovi, Edward Kennedy, Michelangelo, Liza Minnelli, Elizabeth Taylor, and Carrie Underwood.

On the whole, Pisces people usually have a strong appetite because their sense of taste and smell is very acute. They like a variety of foods because they have changeable eating habits. Pisceans are also known to overindulge in food and drink because they can attract the good life. They are fond of stews, sauces, sweets, and ice cream. Being a water sign, they love seafood. Pisceans need to establish moderation in their diet. They are junk food eaters, which causes overweight issues.

Pisceans benefit from eating a high-protein diet because they have a low metabolism and sluggish digestion system. Lean broiled meat, poultry, all types of seafood, cheeses, and nuts are foods that are high in protein. Pisces people should be careful not to use too much table salt because they are vulnerable to water retention in the body. Melons, watercress, celery, cucumber, and carrots are some foods that help prevent water retention.

Blood circulation in the feet is essential to Pisces individuals. Brain food is also suitable for Pisceans because they are so sensitive to stimuli surrounding them. Lamb, onions, whole-grain cereals, prunes, lemons, oranges, apples, grapes, and dark green leafy vegetables are good for blood circulation and the brain. Blackberries, watermelon, and olives are other foods good for circulation. Foods high in Omega-3 fatty acids such as eggs, fish, avocado, walnuts, and pumpkin seeds are also good for the brain.

The mineral associated with Pisces is Ferrum phosphate. It is iron that aids in manufacturing hemoglobin, an important element in the red blood cell. It transports oxygen from the lungs to other body cells. Anemia, low blood pressure, and inflammation are symptoms of lack of iron in the body. Eggs, barley, liver, collards, dandelion, dried beans, beet tops, kale, lettuce, peas, spinach, sweet potatoes, dates, figs, raisins, prunes, dried fruit, prunes, and strawberries are foods rich in iron.

Because of their ever-changing tastes and desires, Pisces people like various herbs and spices. Rosemary is an excellent herb for Pisces because it can keep them grounded and centered. It gives Pisces a closer connection to the physical realm they desperately need. Anise, caraway, cardamom, cinnamon, fennel, lemongrass, mint, and nutmeg can help the Pisces sluggish digestive system. Parsley helps prevent water retention. Basil is good for blood circulation and the brain. Cayenne, clove, and ginger are good for blood circulation, and Peppermint and sage are good for the brain. Other herbs and spices that bring variety to a Pisces life are curries, garlic, horseradish, mustard, oregano, sweet pepper, thyme, and vanilla.

Pisces people need to drink a lot of water for detoxification. Like Aquarians, coffee can overstimulate them. They should drink herbal teas and caffeine-free drinks. Because Pisces people are very sensitive, they should not drink alcohol. They can end up "drinking like a fish" and become alcoholics.

Pisceans like chocolate. Like Aquarians, they should not overdo it with sweets because of their sensitive bodies. Pisces should eat light, wispy desserts.

Pisces people are great to have for dinner. They like to help out.

Pisces Food Guide

Fish

Anchovy
Bass
Bluefish
Carp
Catfish
Cod
Flounder
Grouper
Haddock
Halibut
Herring
Mackerel
Mahi-mahi
Monkfish
Ocean Perch
Orange Roughy
Red Snapper
Sablefish
Salmon
Sardine
Sea Bass
Shark
Smelt
Snapper
Sole
Sturgeon
Swordfish
Trout
Tuna
Turbot
Whitefish
Yellowtail

Seafood

Caviar
Clams
Crab
Crayfish
Lobster
Mussels
Octopus
Oysters
Scallops
Shrimp
Squid

Meat

Lean Red Meats
Liver
Veal
Venison

Poultry

Capon
Chicken
Cornish Game Hen
Duck
Goose
Pheasant
Quail
Turkey

Beans (High Carbohydrates)

Black-eyed Peas
Cannellini Beans
Chickpeas
Fava Beans
Garbanzo Beans
Great Northern Beans
Green Peas
Kidney
Lentils
Lima Beans
Navy Beans
Pinto Beans
Red Beans
Split Peas
White Beans

Grains/Breads/Cereals/Pastas

Amaranth
Barley
Bran
Brown Rice
Millet
Oats
Pumpernickel
Rye
Wheat
Wheat Germ

Whole-Grain Foods

Buckwheat
Kamut
Spelt
Tabbouleh
Whole Wheat

Cheese/Dairy Products

Butter
Cheeses (low fat)
Cream (low fat)
Eggs
Milk (low fat)
Sour Cream (low fat)
Yogurt (low fat)

Oils

Coconut Oil
Fish Oil
Flax Seed Oil
Olive Oil
Peanut Oil
Safflower Oil
Sesame Oil
Vegetable Oil
Wheat Germ Oil

Vegetables

Alfalfa Sprouts
Artichokes
Arugula
Asparagus
Bean Sprouts
Beets
Beet Greens
Broccoli
Brussels Sprouts
Cabbage
Cauliflower
Carrots
Celery
Collard Greens
Corn
Cucumbers
Dandelion Greens
Eggplant
Endive
Green Beans
Hops
Kale
Leeks
Lettuces
Mushrooms
Mustard Beans
Okra
Onions
Parsnip
Peppers
Potatoes
Pumpkin
Radish
Spinach
Squash
Swiss Chard
Turnip
Turnip Greens
Watercress
Wax Beans
White Beets
Yellow Beans
Zucchini

Fruit

Apples
Apricots
Avocados
Bananas
Blackberries
Blueberries
Mango
Melons
Raspberries
Strawberries
Tangerines
Tomatoes
Figs
Grapes
Grapefruit
Lemon
Lime
Mandarins
Prunes
Raisinsoconut
Cranberries
Dates
Dried Fruit
Peaches
Pears
Plums
Pineapple
Pomegranate
Boysenberries
Cherries
Nectarines
Olives
Oranges
Papaya

Herbs and Spices

Anise
Basil
Cardamom
Caraway
Cayenne
Chile pepper
Cinnamon
Cilantro
Clove
Nutmeg
Cumin
Curry
Fennel
Garlic
Ginger
Horseradish
Lemongrass
Mint
Mustard
Oregano
Parsley
Peppermint
Rosemary
Sage
Sweet Pepper
Thyme
Vanilla
Coriander

Beverages

Decaffeinated Coffee
Decaffeinated Herbal Tea
Water

Other

All Kinds of Nuts
Pumpkin Seeds

Pisces Food Recipes

Pisces are great food lovers. They have a taste for exotic and a wide variety of food items. They easily adapt to different food styles.

Liver and Onions

Serves 4 to 6

1 lb calves' liver

1 medium onion, cut into large pieces

3 Tbsp extra-virgin olive oil

¼ cup flour

1 tsp pepper

¼ tsp garlic powder

Water

Place the flour in a bowl. Flour the pieces of liver and set aside on wax paper.

Heat the oil in a large skillet over medium heat. Add the floured liver pieces and brown on each side. Remove from pan.

Add the onion and garlic powder to the skillet. Sauté the onion for 4 to 5 minutes. Onion should be clear. Add flour, one tablespoon at a time, until the oil is absorbed and the flour is lightly browned. Add water to the flour and onion mixture until it reaches a gravy consistency. Simmer for 5 minutes. Return liver to pan. Cover and simmer for an additional 10 to 15 minutes.

Pepper Steak

Serves 4 to 6

1 lb sirloin, cut in cubes

2 Tbsp butter or margarine

½ cup soy sauce

1½ cups water

2 medium onions, cut in strips

2 bell peppers, cut in strips

2 Tbsp cornstarch

Rice

Melt the butter or margarine in a large skillet over medium heat. Add the sirloin and brown for 10 minutes. Sirloin should be tender. Add the soy sauce and water. Simmer for 10 minutes. Add the onions. Simmer for 5 minutes. Add the bell peppers. Cook until tender. Add the cornstarch to thicken.

Prepare the rice according to package directions.

Serve the sirloin over the rice.

Breaded Tilapia

Serves 4

4 tilapia fillets

½ cup Panko bread crumbs or yellow cornmeal

2 beaten eggs, for dipping

Salt

Pepper

In a small bowl, add the bread crumbs. In a second small bowl, add the beaten eggs.

Dredge the fillets in the eggs and then dip them into the bread crumbs or cornmeal.

Place the fillets in a large skillet over medium heat. Add the salt and pepper. Cook for 10 to 15 minutes. Fillets should be tender and golden brown.

Seafood Casserole

Serves 6 to 8

1 lb crabmeat

1 lb shrimp

½ cup celery, diced

½ cup green pepper, diced

1 small onion

1 small jar pimentos (optional)

1 can cream of celery soup

Salt

Pepper

8 soda crackers, crumbled

¼ stick butter or margarine

Preheat oven to 400 degrees Fahrenheit.

Add the celery, green pepper, and onion in a large skillet over medium heat. Sauté for 5 minutes. The vegetables should be soft. Add the pimentos if using. Let the mixture cool.

Place the ingredients in a large bowl. Mix well. Add the crumbled crackers. Mix well.

Place the mixture in a 1-quart casserole dish. Dot the mixture with butter.

Bake for 45 minutes.

Shrimp and Grits

Serves 4

½ lb shrimp, peeled

½ cup cooking oil

¼ cup flour

½ yellow onion, chopped

Box of grits

Heat the oil in a large skillet over medium heat. Add the flour. Stir until oil and flour becomes a dark roux. Add the onion, salt, and pepper to the roux. Stir and cook for about 5 minutes. Onion should be softened. Add the peeled shrimp. Cook for 5 minutes. Shrimp should be pink.

Prepare the grits according to package directions.

Put the shrimp over the grits when serving.

Butternut Squash Casserole

Serves 4 to 6

4 cups butternut squash, cooked and mashed

2 Tbsp sugar

1 cup evaporated milk

1 tsp vanilla

2 Tbsp butter

2 large eggs, beaten

½ cup pecans

½ cup brown sugar

2 Tbsp flour

2 Tbsp butter or margarine

Preheat the oven to 350 degrees Fahrenheit.

Cook two butternut squash on a cooked sheet for 1 hour. Remove from oven and allow to cool.

Preheat the oven to 325 degrees Fahrenheit.

Spray a large casserole dish with cooking spray.

After the squash cools, cut in half and take out the seeds. Spoon out the rest of the squash into a bowl. Add the sugar, milk, vanilla, and beaten eggs to the bowl. Mash together the ingredients. Place in the prepared casserole dish.

In another bowl, add the pecans, brown sugar, and flour. Mix well. Melt the butter or margarine and add to the mixture. Stir well. Spread this mixture over the mashed butternut squash.

Cabbage Soup

Serves 12

1 medium head of cabbage, chopped
1 medium onion, chopped
2 stalks celery, chopped
6 cloves garlic, minced
1 cup carrots
6 cups chicken, beef, or vegetable broth
2 Tbsp tomato paste
1 cup green beans
1 cup zucchini or spinach
1 can diced tomatoes
1 tsp basil
1 tsp oregano
¼ tsp garlic salt
¼ tsp parsley
¼ tsp thyme
1 tsp salt
1 tsp pepper

Spray a large pot with nonstick cooking spray. Add the onion, celery, garlic, and carrots. Sauté for 5 minutes. The vegetables should be softened.

Add the broth, tomato paste, cabbage, green beans, basil, oregano, garlic salt, parsley, thyme, salt, and pepper. Simmer for 8 to 10 minutes. The vegetables should be tender.

Add the zucchini or spinach. Simmer for 5 minutes.

Serve with whole-grain bread.

Oyster Stew

Serves 4 to 6

4 Tbsp butter or margarine
1 onion, minced
½ cup celery, minced
2 cups heavy cream
1-pint shucked oysters
¼ tsp cayenne pepper
Salt
Pepper

Heat the butter in a 2-quart saucepan. Add the onion and celery. Sauté for 2 to 3 minutes. Onion should be translucent. Add the milk and heavy cream. Bring to barely a boil. Add the undrained oysters and bring to a boil. When the oysters start to curl at the edges, remove the stew from the heat. Add the cayenne pepper, Worcestershire sauce, salt and pepper.

Serve at once in hot bowls. Serve with buttered toast.

Fruit Salad

Serves 4 to 6

1 30-oz can fruit cocktail, drained

1 apple, cut up in pieces

1 banana

Orange juice, pour to taste

Add the fruit cocktail, apple, and banana into a large bowl. Cover with orange juice.

Chill and serve.

Spinach Strawberry Salad with Almonds

Serves 4

½ cup almonds, slivered

1 large bag baby spinach

1 cup strawberries, quartered

1 Tbsp balsamic vinegar
1 tsp Dijon mustard
1 tsp honey
3 Tbsp extra-virgin olive oil
1 oz soft Goat cheese

Salt

Pepper

Add the almonds in a dry skillet. Cook over low heat. Continuously shake the pan until the almonds are toasted. Remove almonds from the pan to cool.

To make the dressing, add the vinegar, mustard, and honey in a bowl. Mix. Add the oil. Whisk.
In a large bowl, add the spinach, strawberries, almonds, and dressing. Toss to coat. Add salt and pepper to taste.

Top with Goat cheese and serve immediately.

Thai Noodle Salad

Serves 8

12 oz dried vermicelli or angel hair pasta

½ cup soy sauce

½ cup vegetable broth

4 Tbsp peanut butter

2 Tbsp fresh lime juice

4 cloves garlic, minced

1 tsp ginger, minced

½ tsp red pepper, crushed (optional)

3 cups cooked chicken, chopped

3 large carrots, shredded

1 small green pepper, seeded and cut into thin strips

1 small red pepper, seeded and cut into thin strips

1 small yellow pepper, seeded and cut into thin strips

6 green onions, cut diagonally into ½ inch pieces

¾ cup fresh cilantro, chopped

Lime wedges for garnish

Cook the vermicelli or angel hair pasta according to package directions. Set aside.

Add the soy sauce, broth, peanut butter, lime juice, garlic, ginger, and crushed red pepper, if using, to a medium saucepan and cook over medium-low heat until the peanut butter has melted. Add the cooked pasta. Toss so that the pasta is evenly coated. Add the chicken. Stir. Add the carrots, green, red, and yellow peppers, onions, and cilantro.

Before serving, add the lime wedges as garnish.

Cherry Cream Pie

Serves 6

2 graham cracker pie shells

1 lb can crushed pineapple

¼ cup flour

Package orange jello

1 can cherry pie filling

4 sliced bananas

Cool Whip

Add the pineapple to a pot and warm over medium heat. Add the flour. Stir constantly. Add 3 ounces of the orange jello. Dissolve. Cover the saucepan and cool. Add the contents to a large bowl. Add the can of cherry pie filling. Mix. Add the bananas. Mix well. Top with Cool Whip. Refrigerate for at least 4 hours.

Chocolate Meringue Pie

Serves 6

2 12-oz cans evaporated milk

4 egg yolks

1 cup sugar

¼ cup flour

¼ cup cocoa

½ tsp salt

½ cup butter or margarine

1 tsp vanilla

1 10-inch baked pie shell

4 egg whites

½ tsp cream of tartar

½ cup sugar

¼ tsp vanilla

Reserve ¼ cup of the evaporated milk and scald the rest.

In a medium-size bowl, hand whip the egg yolks. Add the sugar, flour, cocoa, salt, and ¼ cup of the reserved milk. Whip until smooth. Slowly add the scalded milk. Stir constantly. Add the butter or margarine and return to heat. Cook until thick. Remove from heat. Add the vanilla. If needed, strain through a sieve.

Pour into 10-inch baked pie shell.

Top with meringue. Seal the edge of the curst. Brown for 10 minutes.

To make the meringue, put the egg whites and cream of tartar into a bowl. Beat until foamy. Add 1 tablespoon of sugar at a time to the bowl. Beat until stiff and shiny. Add vanilla. Beat.

Ice Cream Jello Pie

Serves 6

1 graham cracker crust pie shell

1 package strawberry jello

1 package frozen strawberries

1 cup boiling water

1 pint vanilla ice cream

Thaw the frozen strawberries.

In a large saucepan, dissolve the jello in boiling water. Add the juice from the thawed strawberries. Add the ice cream. Stir until melted. Add the strawberries. Stir. Chill in refrigerator until it is a soft jello.

Pour in graham cracker crust pie shell. Chill until firm.

Top with Cool Whip before serving.

Keep refrigerated.

Lemon Pie

Serves 6

1 unbaked, deep pie shell

1 lemon

2 eggs, separated

1 cup sugar

2 Tbsp flour

1 Tbsp butter or margarine, melted

1 cup milk

¼ tsp salt

Preheat oven to 375 degrees Fahrenheit.

Beat the egg yolks.

Grate the rind from the lemon and then juice it into a large bowl. Add the beaten egg yolks, sugar, flour, melted butter or margarine, milk, and salt.

Beat the egg whites stiff. Fold into the mixture. Pour into the pie shell.

Bake for 45 minutes.

ACKNOWLEDGMENTS

I want to thank my late father Harold D. Marks who encouraged me to get in touch with my empathic and psychic abilities. He wanted me to learn to love unconditionally.

I want to thank Robert C. Lape, who introduced me to fine cuisine and epicurean recipes.

Special gratitude goes to Angela Dellafiora Ford whose hard work and creativity made this book possible. I want to thank my editor, Marla McKenna who perfected the manuscript.

I want to thank Markos Papadatos for his unwavering support and encouragement of continuing my spiritual journal and making this book possible

I would also like to acknowledge Mary O'Donohue and Lynn Van Praagh Gratton for endorsing the book.

CREDITS

I would like to give credit to Dreamstime.com, a public vector, for the cover of the book.

I would also like to give credit to publisdomaininvectors.or/en/free-clipart.com for the clip art of the astrological signs.

Food Pictures

Chile
www.widecountry.com/3-delicious-chile-recipes

Roasted Leg of Lamb
https://damndelicious.net/2019/04/06/roasted-leg-of-lamb

Pesto Fettuccini in Plate
Contributor is rezkr at istock.com

Chocolate Fondue with Various Fruits
Contributor is Dream79 at canstock.com

Broccoli and Bacon Muffin Tin Frittatas
Recipe | Cooking Light Cookinglight.com
Meredith Corporation
Copyright 2022

Walnut-Crusted Orange Roughy
www.pininterest.com/orange-roughy/
tasteofhome.com

Asparagus Girl
Contributor is barsik at canstock.com

Strawberries and Cream
Contributor is Cat Coming at pexels.com

Grilled Fish with Fresh Vegetables
Contributor is Kanawa_Studio at istock.com

Carrot Bran Snack Bars

www.pininterest.com/carrotbransnackbars/
infinebalance.com

Nuts
Contributor is Vie Studio at pexels.com

Flank steak
Contributor is Kasumi Loffler at pexels.com

Crab Cake Sandwich
Contributor is Annapolis Studios at istock.com

Tuna Steak
Contributor is RODNAE Production at pexels.com

Angel Food Cake
Contributor is HHLtDave5 at istock.com

Melon Fruit Salad
www.pininterest.com//
Melon Fruit Salad Recipe - The Anthony Kitchen
April 22, 2019

Lamb Chops
Contributor is rudisill at istock.com

Lobster Tail
Contributor is Roman Odintsov at pexels.com

Seared Scallops
Contributor is RODNAE Production at pexels.com

Happy Young Woman Eating a Soup at a Restaurant
Contributor is Wrangler at canstock.com

Oatmeal Cookies
Contributor is cottonbor at pexcls.com

Beef Stew
Contributor is Timur Saglambilek at pexels .com

Escargot
Contributor is Maria Orlova at pexels.com

Mussels
Contributor is fcafotodigital at istock.com

Trifle – Dessert
Stock Photos
Stock photo ID: 873058070
Upload date: November 11, 2017

Chicken Tandoori
Stock Photos
Stock phot ID: 911502736
Upload date: January 28, 2018

Seafood Paella
Contributor is Joshua Miranda at pexels.com

Eggplant Parmesan
Contributor is Zen Chung at pexels.com

Fudge
Julia's musings: Anyone want fudge? - Giveaway!! (juliakoponick.blogspot.com)

Serving Goulash
Contributor is GoodLifeStudio at istock

Pizza
Contributor is Diva Plavalaguna at pexels.com

Stuffed Cabbage Leaves
Contributor is freeskyline istock.com

Sloppy Joe
Contributor is rudisill at istock.com

Lady and Chicken
Contributor is Tim Douglas at pexels.com

Macaroni and Cheese
Contributor is Any Lane at pexels.com

Pancakes
Contributor is RODNAE Productions at pexels.com

Beef with Broccoli and Rice Asian Cuisine
Contributor is Lesyy at istock.com

The BEST Lemon Cookies - Live Well Bake Often

Shrimp and Grits

Contributor is rudisill at istock.com

Butternut Squash
Contributor is Karolina Grabowska at pexels.com

ABOUT THE AUTHORS

Peter Marks

Peter Marks is an acclaimed spiritual adviser, psychic medium, astrologer, media personality, and author who intuitively reads for a wide variety of people from all over the world including celebrities, royalty, CEOs, and all walks of life.

As a 30-year veteran in his field, Marks is known for his spot-on readings while working with his client's spirit guides and astrological natal charts, as well as tuning into his remarkable psychic abilities. He provides his clients with accurate information he receives communicated through signs, visions, and direct conversation. His spirit guides assist him in tuning into his client's life path and potential for fulfilling their spiritual goals and reaching total spiritual well-being.

Peter provides insights on career, love life, family, business, and personal issues, and he is known for his warm, friendly style, and uncanny accuracy. He is a deeply spiritual man and believes that faith is a powerful force that can shape lives and society in positive and productive ways. Peter's clients adore his unique approach and interesting perspective.

In recent years, Marks has been invited to the esteemed Society Room in Hartford, Connecticut to provide his highly sought-after consultations. He has been featured in *Natural Awakenings Magazine*, *Digital Journal*, *The Huffington Post*, *The Jim Masters Show*, *The Joyce Barrie Show*, as well as other media outlets. Peter is also featured in the well-reviewed book, *The Gift Within Us: Intuition, Spirituality and the Power of Our Own Inner Voice,* which includes interviews with accomplished scientists and researchers, as well as some of the world's most talented intuitives.

Recently Peter formed a strategic business alliance, Marks Rybak Global Media, with business partner, Stefan Rybak. The company produces exclusive long-form and short-form video and audio programming content that informs, inspires, motivates, and entertains viewers and listeners, and provides guidance, direction, and enlightenment. Production includes, but is not limited to, podcasts, streaming media, books, and a multimedia platform that provides resources on education, encouragement, entertainment, and self-improvement to a global audience.

You can listen to their new podcast, *Free Psychics Online*, which provides guidance, direction, and enlightenment from some of the world's most gifted psychics, astrologers, and spiritual mediums. Listeners' past, present, and future are explained with positivity, clarity, and love.

In Peter's free time, he enjoys cooking, socializing with friends and family—especially his son Robert—going to the theater, and visiting museums. He also loves researching and exploring astrology and progressions.

Peter lives on his nonworking Connecticut dairy farm and enjoys the nature and beauty that surrounds his beautiful state. For more information, please visit peter-marks.com

Angela Dellafiora Ford

Angela Dellafiora Ford was born and raised in Western Pennsylvania. She received a bachelor's degree in political science from Indiana University of Pennsylvania. For over 32 years, she worked for the Federal Bureau of Investigation (FBI), Army Intelligence, and the Defense Intelligence Agency (DIA) in Washington D.C. For nine of these years, Angela worked for and participated in DIA's psychic phenomenon program, STARGATE, and worked as a remote viewer.

Angela was a psychic consultant for Former Secretary of Defense William S. Cohen's fictional book, *Murder in the Senate.* In June 1999, the Discovery Channel aired a case reenactment that Angela solved for U.S. Customs. Scott Carmichael, a former DIA investigator, wrote a Kindle book titled *Unconventional Method.* It describes how Angela used her abilities and helped him catch an Australian spy. Annie Jacobsen wrote about Angela in her book *Phenomena,* published in 2017. Angela appeared on CBS Sunday Morning on March 18, 2018, and August 19, 2018

In December 2015, Angela was invited to Moscow by the official Russian newspaper *Rossiyskaya Gazeta* to attend a reception in honor of two books about the U.S. and Soviet psychic programs. Her work appears in both books. During her stay, she appeared on two Russian television programs.

www.ingramcontent.com/pod-product-compliance
Lightning Source LLC
LaVergne TN
LVHW080846170826
845678LV00006B/1727

* 9 7 8 1 9 4 5 9 0 7 9 6 8 *